Further Materials on
# Lewis Wetzel
and the
## Upper Ohio Frontier

The Historical Narrative of George Edgington
Peter Henry's Account
The Narrative of Spencer Records
The Reminiscences of Stephen Burkham

Edited by
*Jared C. Lobdell*

Published for the Draper Society

HERITAGE BOOKS
2007

# HERITAGE BOOKS
*AN IMPRINT OF HERITAGE BOOKS, INC.*

**Books, CDs, and more—Worldwide**

For our listing of thousands of titles see our website
at
www.heritagebooks.com

Published 2007 by
HERITAGE BOOKS, INC.
Publishing Division
65 East Main Street
Westminster, Maryland 21157-5026

Copyright © 1994 Jared C. Lobdell

Other books by the author:

*Action at the Galudoghson, December 14, 1742: Colonel James Patton, Captain John McDowell and the First Battle with the Indians in the Valley of Virginia with an Appendix Containing Early Accounts of the Battle*

*Indian Warfare in Western Pennsylvania and North West Virginia at the Time of the American Revolution, Including the Narrative of Indian and Tory Depredations by John Crawford, the Military Reminiscences of Captain Henry Jolly, and the Narrative of Lydia Boggs Shepherd Cruger*

*Recollections of Lewis Bonnett, Jr. (1778-1850) and the Bonnett and Wetzel Families*

All rights reserved. No part of this book may be reproduced or transmitted in any form or by any means, electronic or mechanical, including photocopying, recording or by any information storage and retrieval system without written permission from the author, except for the inclusion of brief quotations in a review.

International Standard Book Number: 978-0-7884-0073-8

# TABLE OF CONTENTS

**INTRODUCTION** ........................................................................................... v
  Peter Henry's Account ................................................................... viii
  The Spencer Records Narrative ............................................................ x
  Stephen Burkam ............................................................................ xi

**I. THE HISTORICAL NARRATIVE
OF GEORGE EDGINGTON** ....................................................... 1
  The Edgington Family ..................................................................... 1
  Captivity of Thomas Edgington ............................................................ 2
  Dunmore's War ............................................................................ 3
  Foreman's Grave Creek Affair ............................................................. 3
  Captain Samuel Mason ..................................................................... 3
  Crawford's Campaign ...................................................................... 4
  The Second Attack on Wheeling ............................................................ 5
  The Attack on Rice's Blockhouse .......................................................... 7
  The Wetzels .............................................................................. 7
  The Capture of Lewis and Jacob Wetzel .................................................... 8
  Lewis Wetzel ............................................................................. 9
  Jacob Wetzel ............................................................................ 13
  The Death of George Wetzel .............................................................. 14
  The Death of John Wetzel, Senior ........................................................ 15
  The Poes ................................................................................ 16
  Other Frontiersmen: Ned Sherlock ........................................................ 18
  Other Frontiersmen: Fitch, Stevenson, Williamson ........................................ 18
  Simon Girty ............................................................................. 19
  John Bingaman ........................................................................... 19
  Captain Samuel Brady .................................................................... 20
  Blockhouse Attacks ...................................................................... 22
  McMahon's Scout ......................................................................... 23
  McCulloch's Scout ....................................................................... 23
  Van Buskirk Killed ...................................................................... 25
  The Beaver Blockhouse Affair -- 1791 .................................................... 26
  The Crow Family ......................................................................... 28
  The Johnson Boys ........................................................................ 28

**II. PETER HENRY'S ACCOUNT OF HIS
CAPTIVITY AND OTHER EVENTS** ........................................ 29
  Letter of Robert Orr to Lyman Copeland Draper ........................................... 29
  Peter Henry's Answers to Lyman Draper's Questions ....................................... 31

Peter Henry's Account of His Capture and Other Events ....................35
Of Captain Samuel Brady ................................................................43
Of Major Wilson..............................................................................45
Other Experiences............................................................................47

## III. THE NARRATIVE OF CAPTAIN SPENCER RECORDS ....................51
Introductory ....................................................................................51
Appendix.........................................................................................86
Appendix No. 1................................................................................87
Appendix No. 2................................................................................87
Appendix No. 3................................................................................88
Additions.........................................................................................90

## IV. THE REMINISCENCES OF STEPHEN BURKAM ....................91
Williamson's Moravian Campaign....................................................92
Crawford's Campaign......................................................................93
First Siege of Wheeling ...................................................................94
Lewis Wetzel...................................................................................94
Ben Ulin..........................................................................................95
Second Siege of Wheeling ...............................................................95

## APPENDIX I: PETER HENRY'S OTHER NARRATIVE ....................99

## APPENDIX II: RECOLLECTIONS OF RACHAEL JOHNSON ....................103
Before the Revolution......................................................................103
First Siege of Wheeling ...................................................................104
Foreman's Defeat............................................................................105
Second Siege of Wheeling ...............................................................105
Other Information ...........................................................................106

## INDEX ....................107

# INTRODUCTION

This volume concludes the Draper Society's first series of materials relating to the Warfare on the Upper Ohio, between the end of the French and Indian War (1754-1763) and Anthony Wayne's victory at Fallen Timbers (1794). The first volume presented the memoirs of Lewis Bonnett, Jr., concerning Lewis Wetzel and the Bonnett and Wetzel families. The second included the military reminiscences of Captain Henry Jolly, covering the years 1775-1794, the narrative of Mrs. Lydia Boggs Shepherd Cruger, covering principally the Second Siege of Wheeling in 1782, and the narrative of Indian and Tory depradations in southwestern Pennsylvania, principally in 1777, written by John Crawford. Captain Jolly and Mrs. Cruger both include material on Lewis Wetzel, and their accounts are virtually the only recollections of the attack directed at what is now Washington, Pennsylvania, in 1781.

In the first two volumes of the series, the introductions provided an overview of the move westward in the 1760s and 1770s, and of the Ohio Country at the beginning of the American Revolution. The reader is referred to those volumes for that overview. This introduction attempts to relate the narratives to each other, and to some extent to those in the first two volumes, but it assumes some background knowledge -- which, of course, need not have been gained from the first two volumes.

The first (historical) narrative is that by George Edgington, already mentioned in Bonnett's recollections. The narrative was taken down in three installments by Lyman Copeland Draper, in 1845. It was Edgington who arranged for the naming of Wetzel County, Virginia (now West Virginia). His own experience was mostly at Holliday's Cove Fort, upriver from Wheeling, and his narrative of Wetzel and the Wetzel family is notably incorrect in several particulars -- most notably on George Wetzel's death, which he misdates. But the narrative is certainly not without value: indeed, to put it that way is itself somewhat ungenerous.

For one thing, Edgington devotes equal time to Wetzel and to Samuel Brady, the other great scout of the time, whose sphere of operations was generally northward of Wetzel's, and who was a Captain of Spies, not a pathological individualist (for such Wetzel appears to have been). His narrative is thus characterized by an attempt at balance and a wider view than Bonnett's first-hand but family-oriented reminiscence. For another, this is one of the few accounts to consider the scouts out toward present-day Zanesville, Ohio, in the 1790s -- which was the period of Edgington's own service, and of which, indeed, he provides one of the better accounts. For yet another, there are no other memoirs from the Holliday's Cove community (at least that I have found).

Essentially, Edgington is in the tradition of Joseph Doddridge (1769-1826) and John Crawford (1772-1831). On a base of limited personal experience but long exposure to frontier traditions, he tried to build an account reconciling the different traditions and making use of personal experience. Unlike Doddridge and Crawford, he never (so far as we know) wrote his account down, but like them, he tended to focus on events that were prominent in general frontier recollections, along with those in which, to some degree, he or members of his family participated. After 1780, these were downstream from Pittsburgh (Fort Pitt), though it must be remembered that downstream is first north, then northwest, then west, then southwest of the Pittsburgh settlement, because of the way the Ohio River flows from the confluence of the Monongahela and Allegheny.

Thomas Edgington came from Hampshire County, Virginia, with his young son, in 1771, settling on Redstone Creek, and then, in 1780, to Holliday's Cove, on the (West) Virginia shore, a short distance above the present city of Steubenville, Ohio, now is.

He worked hard with others in rebuilding the fort at Holliday's Cove, which had been accidentally burnt in 1779 -- set on fire when it was unoccupied. During the rebuilding, he went to the fort, but three miles from home and not over four miles and a half above Steubenville -- to get a swingletree he had left there. He was beset a mile on his way and captured. The same party of Indians went to the Cove Fort, where but a single family resided, and had they known the weakness of the fort, they could easily have taken it, as George Edgington notes.

One of the interesting items in Edgington's narrative is his account of Samuel Mason, who "settled early on Wheeling Creek with a bad name from the start -- [a] horse thief." This is the Samuel Mason who plays a leading part in Robert Coates's *The Devil's Trace* (1930), that curious product of the same Yale College renascence that produced Stephen Benet's *John Brown's Body* (1929) and Thornton Wilder's *Bridge of San Luis Rey*,

INTRODUCTION vii

operating through a sense that the key to the character of the Americas can be found in the reconstruction of specific historical attitudes and historical events.

On the vexed question of Betty Zane's exploit, Edgington (without having been at the 1782 Siege of Wheeling) comes down firmly on the Zane side, as against Lydia Boggs Shepherd Cruger and Molly Scott. Here is what he says: "Four or five families were quartered of nights in Zane's Blockhouse. The women in the fort, lead getting scarce, run up pewter spoons, and this failing, called out to those in the blockhouse to bring some powder and lead. None ventured to go. Miss Zane said she would, filled from the keg her apron with powder and lead and run from the blockhouse to the fort, amid a shower of bullets."

Edgington's account of the attack on Rice's Fort (which he calls Rice's Blockhouse) should be amended by appeal to the documents printed in Raymond Bell's 1984 *The Dutch Fork Settlement of Donegal Township, Washington County, Pennsylvania* (Washington, PA), one of a number of Professor Bell's monographs and pamphlets that I believe deserve a collected reprinting.

On Lewis Wetzel, the most interesting parts of Edgington's accounts are those dealing with Wetzel in New Orleans and the time after, and with David Bradford's involvement with Wetzel, which suggests some connection between the two in the Whiskey Rebellion days. On what happened to Wetzel after he finally left Wheeling, here is what Edgington says: he "was now over [left blank] and probably irksome, went to the west, and probably became connected with the upper garrison, five or six hundred miles above St. Louis, and there died aged [left blank], probably a hunter to the last."

There is an account of the Poe brothers' famous fight, with this interesting note: Andrew Poe "was six feet two inches, raw boned, and would weigh 225 pounds -- in his old age considerably exceeded 300 pounds. He died, not many years since [as of 1845], near Beavertown, Pennsylvania."

One of the Indians killed in the canoe in the Poes' battle, at Montour's Run, 6 miles below Pittsburgh, August 17, 1780, floated down and lodged on Brown's Island, opposite Holliday's Cove Fort. George Edgington, then a boy, got the skull, and an ingenious mechanic got the finger bones, and proposed making knife and fork handles of them, which his wife vetoed.

In the summer of 1781, Samuel Brady commanded Holliday's Cove Fort, with his company of fifty men. From this time, besides Brady's romance with Captain Van Swearingen's daughter, Edgington reports the following statement, which contrasts with the attitudes of (for example) Lewis Wetzel: "I have lost a kind father and affectionate brother at their hands, and I have not went farther in search of revenge than any man had gone, as far as any man could go, or any man dare go, but I would scorn to kill an Indian in time of peace, nor women and children in time of war or peace."

Edgington gives us an account of the blockhouses below Pittsburgh on the western bank of the Ohio, around 1790, which is worth noting here. Opposite Wheeling Island, was Lt. Joseph Biggs, with twenty men, engaged in building a new blockhouse: they were attacked in the spring of 1791. Next above the Wheeling blockhouse was the one a mile below Wellsburg, and Lieutenant Lawrence Van Buskirk commanded, and where Edgington was stationed. Van Buskirk was killed May 10, 1791, according to Edgington, and Edgington and his friend Hugh Brady, Samuel's half-brother, were of the party that went out to meet the Indians. The next blockhouse was Yellow Creek blockhouse, sixteen miles above what is Steubenville. Captain Forbes had a Pennsylvania company stationed there, shortly before Van Buskirk was killed.

Hugh Brady (1768-1851) is worth mentioning not only as George Edgington's friend and Samuel's brother, but as an officer in Wayne's Legion, and at the time of his death in Michigan in 1851, Brevet Major General Hugh Brady, still on active duty at eighty-three.

Edgington also, as noted, gives accounts of some of the scouts out toward Zanesville. These include Major William McMahon in the fall of 1792, with a scout of some sixty men; when they reached where Zanesville now is, they divided, and two scouts were sent out, McMahon leading one up Owl Creek, and Thomas Edgington (George's father) headed the other. Similarly, Captain John McCulloch and Lieutenant Joseph Biggs with a scout of sixty men went to the same place -- and there McCulloch divided the men, leading one party against the camp, while Biggs led the other, on one of the head branches of Owl Creek.

PETER HENRY'S ACCOUNT

The reminiscences of Peter Henry are of a different sort. Henry, aged nine, was captured with his sister Margaret by Indians that massacred the remainder of the family, except for his absent father. This was in 1779, and there is an account of their rescue, written by Henry Jolly, in the previous volume of this series. An alternative account, taken down by Samuel Rea in

INTRODUCTION    ix

1855, is in Draper MS 12E: 254-257, and is published in Louise Phelps Kellogg, *Frontier Advance on the Upper Ohio* (Madison 1916), and reprinted in Appendix II here. There is also a brief reminiscence by Margaret Henry in Draper 8NN67, partially printed here.

In the edition of Henry's Account given here, I have decided not to combine the Rea version (printed as an appendix), Peter Henry's answers to Lyman Draper's questions, and this longer Orr version into a single narrative. That kind of combination was the procedure followed in Lewis Bonnett's Narrative, the first book in this series, where the letters answering Draper's questions were much longer than the original narrative. Here there are twenty-eight questions and two versions of the Account. But the answers to the questions are brief, and the chief difference between the two versions of the Account lies in the additional material in the Orr version ("Peter Henry's Account of His Capture and Other Events") -- as, for example, with the material on Wallis's Fort on the Kiskiminetas (then Westmoreland County), which also appears in the answer to Question 28.

Peter Henry's brief captivity took place in the area of the Kiskiminetas and ended at the mouth of the Mahoning. This is an area north and northeast and east of Pittsburgh, in what was then and is now Pennsylvania, whereas Edgington's Narrative concerns (West) Virginia. The Spencer Records Narrative covers Southwestern Pennsylvania (much of it in the Redstone Country) and then Kentucky, and the Reminiscences by Stephen Burkam cover events in (West) Virginia and what is now Ohio.

The "Other Events" include Jacob Smith's account of a Brady scout, as told to Peter Henry, Major Wilson's account of "brushes" with the Indians at Wallis's Fort "on the adjoining farm," or at Colonel Pomeroy's two miles further on, all along the Kiskiminetas, and a mixed bag of other alarms and excursions, tailing off to a brief call-out of the Militia in the War of 1812.

After the War of the Revolution, but before what has been called President Washington's Indian War, Peter Henry "was drafted in Westmoreland County, to serve a two months tour under Captain John Craig and marched with him to what was called Craig's Blockhouse not far from the Town of Shaloeta on Crooked River in Indiana County." He was not eighteen years of age (1788), as he reports, but was willing to go on scout for two months, and while he was at Craig's Blockhouse, an express came from Kirkpatrick's, a few miles off, that the Indians had attacked Kirkpatrick's house there and had killed two or three. About ten or twelve of the men at Craig's volunteered and set off for Kirkpatrick's. Henry's Account gives a good second-hand account of an engagement typical of that lost time.

This version of Peter Henry's Account ends with several two-month tours of duty in the very early 1790s, and, as remarked above, a note on an even briefer tour in the War of 1812. The two-month tours may be set beside the concluding portion of Edgington's Narrative, as well as the Bonnett materials in Volume I of this series, and the concluding bits of Jolly and Mrs. Cruger in Volume II.

THE SPENCER RECORDS NARRATIVE

This is a very different dish of tea from Edgington and Henry, inasmuch as it is a dish brewed with at least limited publication in mind (if only to family members). Spencer Records was born in Sussex County, Delaware, on December 11, 1762, the son of Col. Josiah Records. In 1765 Josiah Records and his family wintered on Antietam Creek, near Hagerstown, and then in 1766 crossed the Alleghenies and settled in the Redstone Country, near the foot of Laurel Hill. There they remained until Josiah Records bought land fourteen miles from Fort Pitt, on the north fork of Robertson's Run.

In 1776, "in an interval of peace" (in the words of Spencer Records), Josiah Records built a mill on Raccoon Creek, ten miles northeast from Robertson's Run, and spent most of the year 1777 there. In 1778, the family forted at McDonald's Fort, two and a half miles from home on Robertson's Run. For these years, and particularly for the years 1780-1782, Records recounts the usual alarms and excursions of the Pennsylvania frontier along the Redstone and Youghiogheny. He also recounts a remark of young Jane Sproul, aged eleven, in 1779: "It is easy to fight Indians, sitting in the chimney corner, with your bellies full of mush and milk" -- though it is true he recounts it in the context of his later adventures in Kentucky.

These accounts of alarms and excursions are ordinary enough -- but listen to the opening of his account of Colonel Williamson's "campaign" against the Moravian Indians: "And it came to pass in those days, that the devil entered into Colonel Williamson (who lived fifteen or twenty miles west of us [at Washington, Pennsylvania]) and stirred him up, to raise a company of men, to go against a town of friendly Indians." This is the Spencer Records speaking who notes later in his Narrative that "as to my political principles [as of 1842], I am a true Whig. The sin of loco-focoism I have never been guilty of. In my religious principles, I am a Regular Baptist, having believed in that doctrine for more than fifty years."

In 1784, Spencer Records went to Kentucky, the same year in which his father moved to Peters Creek. "taking a final leave of the plantation on

Robertson's run." The next year, his father sold the Peters Creek land to Amos Wilson, "on a credit," and came to settle in Kentucky. In 1786, 1787, 1788 -- and then later in 1795 and 1796 -- Spencer made the overland trek back to Pannsylvania, in the first three cases in connection with Mr. Wilson's credit. These trips were taken out of the Indian season: in 1786, there is Indian horse-stealing in Kentucky, and in 1787 Colonel Todd's campaign, both of them recounted briefly here, along with the trips east. The Records family was now settled near Washington, Kentucky.

In 1790 Spencer Records married. At this point he held a Captain's commission in the Militia from the Governor of Virginia, and under this commission he fought the Indians and patrolled the borders in the next two years. In 1792, the commission was re-granted by the Governor of Kentucky, and he held it till 1795. In 1800 he returned to Pennsylvania, and then in 1801 moved to Ohio, from which he moved to Indiana in 1821, where he farmed actively until 1833, at three score years and ten. But the last two score of these years are recounted in very abbreviated fashion. The meat of the Spencer Records Narrative lies in the years from, say, 1780 to 1783 in Pennsylvania, and 1784 to 1792 in Kentucky, with the first three trips back and forth. There are also accounts of how to build a log fort. The Narrative includes information on his children.

STEPHEN BURKAM

Much of the most interesting part of the Reminiscences of Stephen Burkam, from Draper MS 2S: 238-254, has already been excerpted in the four-part account of Crawford's Expedition published in the *Western Pennsylvania Historical Magazine*.

Burkam's father, Solomon, settled near Beason's Fort (now Uniontown) in 1768, so that Stephen Burkam, like his contemporary Spencer Records, was from the Redstone Country. However, his Reminiscences, besides Redstone and Crawford material, also include information on Fort Laurens in 1779, on Williamson's murder of the Moravians, at which (regrettably) he was present, on the Siege of Wheeling in 1782, and on the "Siege" of Rice's Fort, the land land engagement of the War of the Revolution (in Claysville, PA).

Burkam says that "Elizabeth Zane did carry powder at the first siege" (where he was not present, but he "heard many who were there say so"). He adds that "she was not at the second siege" (where he was present). He gives the British/Indian forces at eighty British under Captain Pratt and two hundred Indians under George Girty. Burkam had returned from Stillwater

Creek with Ebenezer and Jonathan Zane on Sunday before the siege began on Wednesday, and he was with the party that went to get two kegs of whiskey that Andrew Zane had hidden on the way back from Catfish Camp (Washington, PA) a few days before. This was on the very day of the attack.

Simon Girty, according to Burkam, sent an express to his brother George, announcing his victory at the Blue Licks, in Kentucky, on the second day of the siege, which information George immediately conveyed to the garrison at Wheeling. (Burkam notes that Dan Sullivan recognized George Girty's voice.)

Burkam gives a slightly different version of the taunting of Betsey Wheat from that given by Lydia Boggs Shepherd Cruger (see the second volume of this series): "Pratt speaks, said he was a Scotchman, closed by wishing no harm. Betsey Wheat and George Girty confabbed. Girty asked if they had whiskey. Yes, plenty of it. How was it made? In a melting ladle, and you shall have a belly full of it. Said Girty, 'I'll have the fort before morning, or go to hell.' 'Hell, then,' said Betsey, 'is your portion, for into the fort you cannot come.' Then commenced a mutual throwing of stones."

In view of a review note on the second volume in this series (suggesting more specific attention be paid to the role of African-Americans on the frontier), I call particular attention to this passage from Burkam:

At Zane's house, "Old Sam," the negro, was slightly grazed. He pulled out his plug and fired out, saying "Take care! Sambo is here!" They kept away from Zane's house the remainder of that night. Next day, they shot at a Negro with the Indians, wounded him, and he surrendered and came in. He had been taken on Clinch, had on Major Harrison's coat, with a bullet hole through it.

In line with this, I think it well to include as a second appendix, the Narrative of Rachael Johnson, an ancient lady of color, supposedly born in Delaware in 1736, who died in 1847. While my experience in editing African-American women's narratives (as in *Sylvia Dubois*, OUP 1988) makes me suspicious of her claimed great age, nevertheless Rachael could have been 109 at the time she was interviewed. Her recollection of George Rogers Clark, if true, is highly illuminating, and she, like Burkam, puts Betty Zane's feat at the 1777 Siege of Wheeling, and Molly Scott at the 1782 Siege. The difference is that she claims to have been present at the first, and not at the second -- which is the reverse of Burkam.

INTRODUCTION    xiii

Though Lyman Draper considered and rejected the hypothesis that Betty Zane's exploit came in 1777, and Molly Scott's in 1782, and finally gave up (as Joseph Doddridge had given up) trying to solve the problem, it seems to me that, if we can trust Rachael's recollection, this "two-siege hypothesis" must be the case, while if we cannot, it is at least as likely that Betty Zane (who was well-known) gained credit for what Molly Scott had done (who was not so well-known) as the other way 'round. But I don't suppose we will ever know the answer, short of Judgment Day. And then it will not matter.

The next Draper Society volumes will turn from the Upper Ohio to Ohio itself (in 1790-91), and also south to the Valley of Virginia and Sandy Creek, in the 1740s and 1750s (and 1760s). But there is still additional material on the Upper Ohio, and we will some day return to that.

My thanks are as before, in the first two volumes, with the addition of Robert Serum of Northwood University, In Midland, Michigan, where I am currently teaching, and where the Draper Society is currently located, though I suspect we will be relocating once again shortly. My renewed thanks to Karen Ackermann and Heritage Books.

Jared Lobdell<br>
Midland, Michigan<br>
October 1993

# THE HISTORICAL NARRATIVE OF GEORGE EDGINGTON

## THE EDGINGTON FAMILY

George Edgington (my informant's grandfather), who came from London to America, and settled first near Philadelphia and there married, then to Hampshire County, Virginia, below the mouth of the South Branch, thirty miles from Winchester. Edwards's Fort, six miles from Edgington's, [was] where the people forted. Edgington went to a tub mill belonging to another Edwards, and there were about a dozen Dutch boys and girls also there at [the] mill and all had to stay over night. [The] next morning, all were taken by the Indians; [they] tomahawked the children (except two boys and Edgington) in the mill, and set it on fire, and started for Fort DuQuesne.

After going three miles, they killed the two remaining Dutch boys. In crossing a stream, an Indian walked over a log, leading Edgington, who waded and when in the middle of the stream pulled in the Indian, who when reaching the shore, aimed a tomahawk blow, which Edgington partly dodging, split his nose and upper lip; the other Indian interfered and saved a repetition of the blow; tied up the wound -- took him first to Fort DuQuesne, then up the Scioto, and kept him three years.

Two days after Edgington was taken, his wife barely escaped being with a couple of families of eight persons, under protection of two soldiers, going to Edwards's Fort; all were waylaid and killed. While he was absent, his wife, two years after, not doubting he was killed at the mill, married again; but when he returned, he kindly gave her the choice of husbands, and she chose her first. [They] emigrated to Western Virginia. Both died, aged --.

D. M. Edgington, son of George, says in conversation that his grandfather, Thomas Edgington, died at Holliday's Cove in 1816. [This] Thomas Edgington (my informant's father) came from Hampshire County, Virginia, and settled in 1771 on Red Stone Creek, in 1780 removed to Holliday's Cove.

## CAPTIVITY OF THOMAS EDGINGTON

The next spring [after the Affair of the Poes and the Half King's Sons -- J.C.L.], Scotash, with a party of ten -- Simon Girty [being] one of them -- captured Thomas Edgington (the father of my informant), [on] the 1st of April 1782. [This is corroborated in Vermont Historical Collections, II, p. 356 -- L.C.D.] [This was] a little before Crawford's Campaign. Mr. Edgington lived on the Virginia shore a short distance above where Steubenville now is. [He] had aided with others in rebuilding the fort at Holliday's Cove, which had been accidentally burnt the year before -- set on fire when unoccupied.

Edgington went to the fort, but three miles from home and not over four miles and a half above Steubenville -- to get a swingletree he had left there. The weather was more [?] fair and [he] desired to plow. When a mile on the way he was beset with Indians and called on to surrender, but he ran and was pursued, [and] jumping a small stream, slipped into the water and got his clothes so saturated with water that he couldn't run to any advantage, and his pursuer still calling out to him to surrender, promising "no kill, no kill," he gave himself up.

This same party at the same time went to the Cove Fort, where but a single family resided, and only two gunmen, one of whom, William Thomas, went out to catch a horse and was killed, and had the Indians known the weakness of the fort, they [could] easily have taken it.

Edgington was well treated by Girty and Scotash, and from them he learned the particulars of the Poe fight, or rather the Indians' side of the story. And both the Poes told the story to my informant, and Dr. Doddridge told him, when reminded of its utter incorrectness, that he got it from an old Pennsylvania magazine, and supposed it true.

The Half King wanted to adopt Edgington in place of one of his sons, but the old Queen was sulky and opposed it, and Edgington expressed [a desire] to be sent to Detroit. He was, after three months with the Indians, sent there and sold.

[See Heckewelder's Historical Account, p. 162, not doubting that Edgington was the person saved from the stake. -- L.C.D.]

Thomas Edgington moved from Redstone to Little Shirtee [Chartiers] in the fall of 1772, having bought 700 acres of excellent land for 160 dollars, of Van Swearingen, who then lived within three miles of Cat Fish's Camp and probably settled there the preceeding spring.

## DUNMORE'S WAR

On the Lower Fork of Yellow Creek, where the Indian town was, a small one; and they concluded to move down the river elsewhere -- stopped at Baker's, drank -- Mrs. Baker told Daniel Greathouse that a squaw told her (in a drunken fit) that the Indians intended to murder Baker's family before leaving. Greathouse went and raised a party of about 30 men -- George Cox, Edward King, and others -- went to Baker's. There an Indian, Logan's brother, was drinking and strutting around in a military coat -- someone shot him and King then stabbed him, while in the agonies of death, saying "Many a deer have I served in this way." Then killed another Indian there, and two squaws -- the two latter shot by Daniel Greathouse and John Sappington. One of the squaws had a child, which was saved and sent to Col. Gibson as its father. Twelve Indians were killed in all. Greathouse died of the measles the following year.

## FOREMAN'S GRAVE CREEK AFFAIR

William Engle escaped the defeat. Tom Brazier, a famous good singer, was engaged in singing going down -- camped over night; and returning, were attacked. Brazier was killed. Jonathan Pugh was taken. Engle ran to Wheeling. Foreman's company was from Hampshire County, Virginia. The dead were left four days before burying them; were eaten by birds and much disfigured and putrid by heat -- swollen and blackened -- none could be distinguished -- stripped, and buried all together. Pugh was gone five years. His father had thought he was killed in the defeat and never knew to the contrary till his son unexpectedly returned and made himself known.

## CAPTAIN SAMUEL MASON

His brother Colonel Isaac Mason settled at the foot of Laurel Hill, above the head of Redstone, as early as 1771 -- [he was] respected. But Captain Samuel did not live there, settled early on Wheeling Creek with a bad name from the start -- [a] horse thief. He had two sons, one John, and two sons-in-law, and all of a feather.

Captain Mason had a singularly Roman hook nose, only equalled by his son John's. Mason lived at the Red Banks -- a party of twenty men started to go and kill him, but he got wind of it and escaped in a skiff, saluted with several long shots. Then he went to the Walnut Hills -- had a party -- waylaid the trails, and would leave from Natchez when a man with a good sum was coming, and lighten his load. If the amount was small, he would not be disturbed.

He was apprehended at New Madrid by Spanish authorities and sent to New Orleans, where it was found no crimes of his could be proven to have been committed in Spanish dominion, and it was determined to send him in irons to the United States, and while conveying him up the river in a boat, and while the men were careless and on shore, he seized a gun and shot the first who approached. The others ran off and thus he regained his liberty. He recommenced his old operations -- captured boats loaded etc. -- reward offered -- two of his men cut off his head. The second said went to Canada.

## CRAWFORD'S CAMPAIGN

[There were] 483 men assembled at the Mingo Town, some three miles below Steubenville, on the Ohio shore (the Mingo tribe left there in 1779), and there were [= were there] some days, getting ready, choosing officers. Crawford had six [votes] majority. Crawford was dejected from the start. The army crossed the Tuscarawas and passed by Mohican John's Lake. The pilots were Thomas Nicholson, John Slover, and Jonathan Zane.

The battle begun on the 4th day of June. The Indians numbered not over 250 -- [They] had sent off their women and children from Upper Sandusky and only expected to retard the whites until all the women and children were fully beyond reach. The Indian spies had seen the men at the Mingo Town, and had twice counted Crawford's men while on the march -- so Thomas Edgington, then a prisoner, learned.

Crawford's men threw their provisions and packsaddles into a heap. Crawford cautioned the men not to pay any attention to dead Indians, thus exposing themselves unnecessarily. During the fight some of the Indians changed their position and ran across a prairie to a piece of timber, and some of the men shot one of the Indians, and Thomas Mills ran off foolishly to get the scalp -- and a large heavy volley of guns was discharged at him just before he reached the dead Indian. He threw himself into the grass; all thought he was killed; he in a few seconds turning himself for retreat, darted up and escaped. This is the same who got killed after returning from the campaign, while with Lewis Wetzel.

Colonel Crawford's son was John -- forty men embodied on the return -- the Indians in one instance found the bodies of two men beside a log with their rifles -- evidently died of starvation.

Slover when a boy had been captured on Montour's Run and kept till a man grown. Visited his people, intending to return, but was gradually persuaded to remain longer and longer, till he finally married and settled. Captain John Biggs, Lieutenant Bladen Ashby, a very handsome young man, and Jacob Boneham (or perhaps another) on return [were] attacked in [the] day, and these three named [were] killed.

Williamson told Crawford, when the Indians took post in the skirt of woods the second day, that they ought to be routed out, but Crawford did not think proper to give Williamson a command to drive them out. [Williamson] asked but 200 men. Crawford wished to keep the men together.

At the first commencement of the fight, [the men] threw the saddles and provisions into a heap, and let the horses go, and the fight commenced about 2 o'clock, p.m., and almost at the first onset four were killed, and several wounded: among the latter were Captain Bane and Joseph Edgington. Dr. Knight attended to the wounded. [They] fought till dark.

The first day Girty rode towards the whites, but was soon driven back; he afterwards said his object was to warn Crawford to retreat while he could.

The next day, the Indians were reinforced by some 1100 Indians -- [they] fought, more or less -- [there was] the Mills incident -- [there was] Williamson's proposition -- In the night Crawford ordered the men to prepare for a retreat, etc. The object of the campaign was not to destroy the balance of the Moraviand, but the Wyandotte towns.

THE SECOND ATTACK ON WHEELING

It was at the first attack ([when Francis] Duke [was] killed) that Mason figured. [The second attack was] July 1782, the latter end of the month [= September -- J.C.L.]. The[y] killed three or four over near the fort, before the presence of the enemy was known. Girty [was there] with between three and four hundred [men]. There was a thicket of pawpaw bushes where the upper part of Wheeling now is (the first fort was near the "point" of Wheeling Creek): the fort in 1782 was on a high bank from the river, and about 200 yards distant from the fort was Zane's Blockhouse. The Indians got into the thicket and fired two days on the fort.

Powder and lead [were] getting short in the fort, and a twenty-five-pound keg of powder and a hundred pounds of lead had been carefully placed away in Colonel Zane's garret for the time of need.

Four or five families were quartered of nights in Zane's Blockhouse. The women in the fort, lead getting scarce, run up pewter spoons, and this failing, called out to those in the blockhouse to bring some powder and lead. None ventured to go. Miss Zane said she would, filled from the keg her apron with powder and lead and run from the blockhouse to the fort, amid a shower of bullets.

Some of the Frenchmen along, went and cut a white oak on the hill, cut off a butt cut of proper length and very tough, split it, gouged out each half, and put them together, and hooped them, and made a cannon. Before they got it ready, two young men who had been sometime prisoners, Moore and Kelly, escaped in the night from the enemy, and gave notice of the cannon, and those within called out, "Come on with your wooden cannon -- we are ready for it!" At daylight next morning they fired it, and it busted all to pieces. They had intended with it to have frightened the fort into a surrender, but Moore and Kelly gave this notice. That day the Indians went off. [There were] thirty-two men in the fort, and five or six at Zane's.

This last day of the siege, John and Samuel McCulloch and Peter Hanks left Van Meter's fort ten miles off from Wheeling, on Short Creek, to go and see if the siege was yet raised, that they might know at Van Meter's what to depend on. As they neared Wheeling, John McCulloch dashing ahead, he met the Indians, some of them approaching him and so near that he had no alternative but to dash down the steep hill a little below the upper end of the wall of the turnpike, and turned his horse down, who mostly slid down on his shanks, and McCulloch still intercepted by Indians between here and the fort, and around the fort made off circuitously and reached Van Meter's almost as soon as Samuel McCulloch and Hanks did -- who, in John's rear, wheeled and escaped from the Indians.

Major John McCulloch kept his faithful old horse -- a brown horse -- many years, and [it] lived to be 34 years old, and [he] fed it latterly on mush, and would not allow it used. My informant has often heard Major McCulloch speak of the leap, and has always so understood it.

The next day John and Samuel McCulloch started from Van Meter's fort for West Liberty fort to give intelligence that the Indians were leaving Wheeling. At Girty's Point, about two miles, Samuel was shot dead beside a sugar maple, and as John ascended the eminence, he turned and saw an Indian in the act of scalping his victim, when John shot him dead and escaped. Samuel was a smart young man, never out in service, just married, and without a commission of any kind. He was killed by a party who first abandoned the siege of Wheeling.

## THE ATTACK ON RICE'S BLOCKHOUSE

A large party of these same Indians who had been at Wheeling went to Rice's Blockhouse, surrounded by several cabins. Rice had gone towards Wheeling for intelligence. At the commencement, the Indians first appeared in a stubblefield and ran up and shot a boy in ascending the ladder in the blockhouse, had his leg broke. Another boy was shot through the head, and a man during the siege was also shot dead, struck in the forehead.

In the afternoon, Rice returned, and attempted to dash in -- and as [he] came to the creek bank (Dutch Fork), here he encountered a large body of Indians under the bank, who shot at him, a ball passing through the flesh part of his leg above his knee, and shooting [his] horse: the animal fell and upon his leg, and he could not disentangle himself, and the Indians were approaching with uplifted tomahawks, when the horse suddenly jumped up and dashed off into the bushes, and fell dead.

When Rice escaped to a neighboring station, three miles off, there got his wound dressed, raised a party of 12 men and put for the relief of his people: as they came about midnight, rather dark star light, with a heavy firing and flashing, the majority of Rice's men were detained. He said he would get in so as to encourage the men -- else they might surrender; and finally two others joined him; the others retreated. Rice and his two companions ran among the Indians without their recognizing them, and nearly reached the blockhouse, when Rice holloawed out. His voice was known. [The] door opened, etc., and the holloawing of Rice and his men led the Indians to think a reinforcement was coming, and they fled.

Before sun down the Indians (about 150 -- Girty with them) set the barn and stable on fire, about 60 yards from the blockhouse, thinking the fire would communicate to the fort -- but fortunately the wind blew the contrary direction. This party retreated by way of Girty's Point, burning grain, etc.

## THE WETZELS

Old John and his boys settled twelve miles up Wheeling at a very early day -- lived by hunting, chiefly. Martin, George, Lewis, Jacob, and John were the order of their ages. Martin and another person were coming from Wheeling fort to Morgan's fort, now Morgantown. Indians waylaid the path and took them prisoners. Wetzel was spared; the other was burned two days before he was dead -- and the second day, Wetzel saw him there sensible, with his bowels hanging out, and [he] wished him when he got in to tell his (the victim's) people of his fate. Wetzel had a beautiful head of hair --

this the Indians cut off. The old Indian who claimed Wetzel killed one of the drinking Indians who had cut his hair off. Wetzel got a horse from the Indians -- this ran away, and Wetzel pursued it to near the mouth of Hocking, caught it, and returned.

A party of six or eight Indians went to Kentucky. Wetzel went along, designing to escape, as he had now been with them nearly two years, and had learned their language, which he desired, and had therefore stayed longer than he otherwise would. When in the neighborhood of Boonesboro, and in the camp keeping sentinel, Wetzel selected his turn near daylight, washed off his paint, and escaped to Boonesboro.

Some were for viewing him as a spy, but Wetzel told them they could keep him in irons until they could ascertain from the Falls of Ohio where he had acquaintances. Seeing things look unfavorably, he was about seizing his gun which he had set down, and run off to the Indians, when Boone, who had been out, appeared and had him well treated, seeing nothing, as he said, improbable in Wetzel's story.

Wetzel remained that season at Boonesboro, hunting and scouting; and once out in a scout, he shot and mortally wounded an Indian, and when he came up to him they recognized each other, and the Indian being shot through the bowels, requested Wetzel to shoot him -- this he declined -- and the Indian was carried till they reached a stream, gave him drink, when he soon sickened and died. Martin then returned to Wheeling.

## THE CAPTURE OF LEWIS AND JACOB WETZEL

While Martin was in captivity, Lewis and Jacob were taken. Their father had taken them (the family in Wheeling fort) to work in the cornfield on Wheeling Creek, and the boys were in the cabin to cook a meal of victuals; and some Indians crept up in the rear of the cabin where the former year was a garden, now thickly grown up to weeds.

Lewis went out to see if his father was coming, when one of the Indians shot him, while Lewis was in the act of turning suddenly, and the ball passed across his breast under the breast bone. Jacob ran off, and the Indian who shot Lewis dropped his gun and took after him, and caught him. Lewis ran, the blood spirting out of his wound and mouth, and was soon overtaken.

When Jacob was taken, he made two attempts to get the Indian's pistol in his belt, but failed. The Indians examined Lewis's wound and thought it doubtful whether he would recover. Their foe then fled to Wheeling [Island?]. The Indians were seven; they had got three horses above on the Creek, and two more at Wetzel's. There were a litter of young dogs at Wetzel's, and one of the Indians selected one and gave it to Jacob to carry -- he threw it into Wheeling Creek, then full. [The] Indians got five guns at Wetzel's.

In crossing the Ohio, two of the horses got their halters off, and returned and got off. On their return [journey], the Indians came to where they had left a deer skin hanging in a tree with some bits of bear meat, "cracklings"; these were maggoty. The Indians ate these, but the boys would not touch any.

The boys -- Lewis 13, Jacob 11 years old -- agreed they would not escape unless they could do so together. [They] camped at Stillwater; the Indians there cooked a raccoon and turkey but never offered the boys any. Lewis being wounded was not tied. Jacob in the night disengaged himself from the fastening by which he was tied to two Indians, when one of them awoke and wanted to know what he was about. [He] said he wanted water. The Indian got him some, and then fastened him and went to sleep.

Again Jacob got loose. Lewis got a gun standing against a tree with a shotpouch, and Jacob pulled another from under the head of one of the Indians, and they got each a pair of moccasins drying on a stick before the fire, and then put off, and it being very dark they made but little progress, and hid till morning in a tree top. Next day they examined the trail and the horsetrack to see that they were going the right way.

[They] struck the Ohio opposite Wheeling Island and made a raft, and put on their rifles, and swam over to the Island. Lewis was so weak from his wound, and had not eaten anything during their captivity and escape -- four days -- [that] he would not have got over but for the assistance of Jacob pushing over their respective rafts.

Old John Wetzel took his sons, Lewis and Jacob, when yet boys, took to Fish Creek on a hunt, and so they should have nothing to eat till they killed something. They went out and found only a wolf, which they brought into camp, cooked, and ate.

LEWIS WETZEL

When Lewis and his father returned from the hunt down at Muskingum, when George was killed, Thomas Mills reached Wheeling with other fugitives. He had, at 19 years old, gone out on Crawford's Campaign, and on return his fine young mare gave out within 18 miles of the river. [He] now engaged Lewis Wetzel to go with him to hunt his horse. While pursuing [the] hunter's path, near where St. Clairsville is [now], [they] met a party of about 40 Indians.

Lewis jumped to tree, as did the Indians. Lewis soon discovered an Indian loading his gun, and [the Indian] exposed his back, and Lewis shot him dead. Then Lewis discovered for the first time that Mills still stood exposed in the path, bewildered and gazing. Lewis wanted him to shoot, but he seemed not to mind what was said to him. Wetzel went to snatch his loaded rifle across his shoulder, but could not get it, and Lewis ran down the trail, loading as he ran. Mills had his cheek grazed, was come up to, and tomahawked.

[Lewis] was pursued. One, a tall Delaware called the Long Pine, with a tomahawk in his hand and a swift runner, pursued while Lewis was loading. Lewis heard his feet patting in the path (Lewis always carried two or three bullets in his mouth, and now put the muzzle of his powder horn to the gun and poured in a goodly quantity, and the ball on top), and by this time, he shouldered his rifle, intending to hasten his speed. The Indian was nearer than Lewis expected and seized the muzzle of Lewis's gun, and they had a tussle, and finally Lewis got the muzzle at a proper level and pulled the trigger and blew the Indian's head nearly to atoms -- and put on. [He] subsequently shot and broke another Indian's thigh -- the latter recovered, but a cripple.

He was still pursued, but gained on his pursuers. All kept the trail, as the nettles and weeds were high and troublesome. Coming to a ridge around which the trail passed, Lewis knew an unfrequented passage by which he went and gained half a mile -- saw no more of the Indians -- ran 12 miles. When he reached the river opposite of Wheeling, not knowing how close his pursuers might be, [he] threw his gun and shotpouch into the weeds, and with his tomahawk he swam over to the island. That was a warm day, and after such a chase he was overheated, and the water chilled him, and he did not get over it for several years. Finally, Dr. Pettee, a Frenchman at Marietta, cured him.

After Wetzel's return, Captain Brady, then stationed at Wheeling, went with a party of twenty men, found Mills's body, stripped and scalped, in the path where killed, [and] buried him. Brady and his men did not find the Indian bodies, but saw where Wetzel had shot the Indian and bespattered a rock beside the path with the brains and blood. Brady and his party, after burying Mills, returned to Wheeling the same night.

At Fort Harmar some little treaty was held, at which Lewis Wetzel was present. Someone told the Indian that Wetzel was one of the boys that had escaped from him and his party. [The] Indian was incredulous, said those boys must have perished. Finally the Indian bethought himself to examine Wetzel's breast and found the scar. Then the Indian was persuaded and professed sincere joy and friendship, and invited, before he left, Wetzel to accompany him home. This must have [been] before 1789. [He] went and was gone about a year and finally returned by himself to the Old Mingo Town, and down to Wheeling.

While he [and] Vachel Dickerson were out spying, with orders not to go further than 10 miles over the Ohio -- but they went to the Muskingum, pretty well up, and discovered an Indian on his way to Marietta, where was quite an encampment of Indians there on a trading visit -- Lewis and Dickerson fired and mortally wounded him, but being mounted, he escaped and died soon after reaching the Indian camp a mile from Fort Harmar. Lewis now visited his sister opposite Marietta on the Virginia side of the river, where he made no secret of his having shot an Indian.

Col. Strong sent a file of soldiers over the river, took him, ironed him, and took him to the fort. In the evening, about sun down, he desired his two guards to let him go out. They had him ironed and each of them were ironed, and finally Lewis got their consent. But he dodged them and ran off into the bushes, and dodged into a tree top.

Several times some in search of him passed very near him. Early next morning, Lewis went to the river, saw his brother-in-law opposite issuing from his cabin. Lewis made signs with his hat. [His brother-in-law] came over with a canoe and took him over, and knocked off his irons. Here Lewis got his rifle, and he felt once more like a free man, but swore he would shoot Col. Strong if ever he got the chance.

For safety he put down the river to Limestone. There one day, when in the tavern, a party of soldiers happened to call there, apprehended him before he knew it, but [he] was subsequently liberated. After this, Lewis came up the river. [He] was with Brady in spring of 1791 at the fight at the Beaver Block House -- and spied along the frontier. He was under Brady's orders when, with Dickerson, he shot the Indian up Muskingum.

About 1790, one Madison with a party went to surveying lands on Big Sandy, and engaged Wetzel to hunt and keep camp for him a little up Sandy on the lower side of Sandy, and promised him 1000 acres of land for that season -- then fall -- till next spring. One day Madison and Wetzel went to a pond some distance off to see some beaver traps Madison had set there -- the pond on the opposite side of Sandy and a mile or two above. Not thinking of danger, they were talking along, and were waylaid and Madison shot dead. Lewis treed and shot an Indian, and then retreated loading as he ran, and before reaching the canoe killed his third Indian and escaped.

Some three or four years after Lewis and Jacob were captured, and Lewis had nearly got his growth, while forted at Wheeling in 1781, Col. Brodhead with his troops halted some time at Wheeling, and two Indians came there in a friendly manner to see Brodhead, and Lewis Wetzel conceived that one of them was of the party that captured him and his brother, but Jacob said not. Lewis contended that he was, and he would kill him.

Someone told Brodhead that if the Indians were not taken care of, that the country people would kill them. So the Colonel had them placed in the guardhouse for safety -- and when one of the guards opened the door to take in some food for them, Lewis slipped in with his tomahawk concealed under his hunting shirt, and drove the blade to the handle -- and the other Indian held down his head meekly to receive the expected blow, which he would have received, but that Wetzel could not get the tomahawk from the Indian's head.

Lewis escaped. Brodhead tried to find out who committed the deed, but none would betray him. The tomahawk was sent around the fort for an owner. None then claimed it. It was left with Colonel Ebenezer Zane. In the fall Lewis claimed it as he was going out on a fall hunt on Stillwater.

Thus Lewis Wetzel killed eight Indians -- not twenty-seven as Doddridge says.

He went down the river as a flatboatsman -- stopped in the neighborhood of the Walnut Hills. Lewis had been engaged to hunt up Benjamin Piatt, who had killed two Indians and when apprehended stabbed and killed the Constable and fled to the canebreaks. Lewis made it his home at an old Frenchman's, and one day while the man and his wife were absent and Lewis was left to take care of the children, he happened to find a pair of dies for counterfeiting dollars. Lewis took some pewter and ran some and gave them to the children. When the Frenchman returned and discovered what Lewis had been doing, in a pet he went and complained at Natchez for making counterfeit money.

The Governor had him arrested and sent him in irons to New Orleans, and there confined him in a dungeon, in irons and without clothing. And there kept him for some years. A petition was sent down to the Spanish Governor for Wetzel's liberation, but no notice was taken of it.

[They] then petitioned President Washington to interfere, but before this latter could be expected, David Bradford, who after the Whiskey War had fled to New Orleans, there became intimate with [the] Governor and begged the liberation of Wetzel. This the Governor agreed to do, saying, however, that he would have to report him dead, and that Wetzel must instantly leave the Spanish dominions.

Lewis was thereupon liberated, a new suit given him, and he walked up to Natchez on foot, thence up the river, visited around the Wheeling region -- was now over [--] and probably irksome, went to the west, and probably became connected with the upper garrison, five or six hundred miles above St. Louis, and there died aged --, probably a hunter to the last.

Major McGuire, of Buffalo Creek, while Lewis was in captivity, was at New Orleans with flan, and offered $2000 for Wetzel's liberation. Richard Brown, of Holliday's Cove, also down with a boat of flour, and Phil Doddridge was along with Brown, and Brown offered $1000, but these bribes did not prove successful, and McGuire came well nigh being himself imprisoned by stealing an interview with Wetzel.

David Bradford settled finally at the Bayou Lara, and there drank himself to death. His family joined him there, and there got a large Spanish grant of land. He was officially pardoned by John Adams, but remained at Bayou Lara, as his Pennsylvania property was then sold and his family was on the way down the river, and he passed them by land, and returned to Pennsylvania, but went back to Bayou Lara. [?Sara]

The old cross-fire story [about Lewis Wetzel], so far at least as the mouth of Short Creek is concerned, my informant thinks cannot have been so, as he would have known it. [He] discredits the "turkey story" at the Indian rock.

## JACOB WETZEL

Jacob Wetzel happened at Mayville when Kenton had raised a party of 30 men, going to pursue Indians who had been stealing horses, went over the Ohio some 60 miles. When Wetzel and Cornelius Washburn (raised on Pigeon in Washington County, Pennsylvania, moved to Kentucky) discovered a hobbled horse on the trail, and concluded he had strayed off, and an Indian would come for him; Wetzel and Wetzel watched till the Indian came and mounted, when they shot and killed him. Kenton sent Wetzel forward, and he discovered a large Indian camp, on a ridge of land between a pond and a creek.

[He] returned and reported that he thought the number too large for Kenton's party, about 60 or 70, some squaws and children among them -- with tents (which they had probably got at St. Clair's Defeat) -- but it being dark he could not tell definitely. It was arranged to steal up [to] the camp and fire upon it at daybreak next morning. This was done and the Indians scattered yelling in every direction, and Wetzel followed some over the creek, waist deep, and found himself surrounded by Indians, treed all around him. But being dressed something like them, they did not discover the mistake till he shot one of them dead a few feet from him, when several fell upon him, and a stroke across his left arm broke it.

He fled. Kenton's men had all gone, and Wetzel had to make the best of his way alone. When out of the reach of the Indians, he stripped off some slippery elm bark and bound it on, first placing the bones as well as he could. In time his arm got well, but ever after crooked. About ten o'clock he overtook one of the fugitives limping along, who had sprained his ankle, and got Wetzel to carry his rifle into Limestone, which he did, disabled as he was, killed a turkey on the way, and ate some raw. Kenton got in first.

Prior to this, Jacob Wetzel and some others took a boat and went from Limestone to kill turkeys on the Indian shore, in the bottom; and after killing some turkeys, discovered two Indians on a raft about a mile below, crossing over to the south side. Wetzel ran down and got a shot with his light load, then reloaded, shot, and tumbled off an Indian, his arms fast in between the poles of the raft. By this time the canoe came with the others of Wetzel's party, and made after the other Indian, who had abandoned his raft and was swimming. When they came quite near him, he would dive, and before they got a chance to knock him in the head, they were fired on by a large Indian party on the southern shore, who previously crossed and now came to the relief of their companion, and they had to put off, and the Indian thus escaped. Jacob Wetzel got the scalp of the one killed.

### THE DEATH OF GEORGE WETZEL

While Crawford was out on his campaign, John Wetzel concluded it would be safe to take a hunt on the Muskingum -- George and Lewis Wetzel, and one Miller -- four in all. [They were] at the island above Marietta, at what is called the Long Reach. Sometime before, a small ship had been built on the Monongahela and loaded with flour for New Orleans, the first attempt of the kind, owned and commanded by Joseph Parkinson, late of Parkinson's Ferry on the Monongahela. At this island this ship ran on a sand bar. They had seen a canoe floating above, which they went and got, and lightened their vessel, got it off, and reloaded. It was then night, and they concluded to stay till morning.

A party of Indians stole up in the night and placed themselves under the bow, and next morning the first white man that showed himself was shot; and so the second; when the Indians called out, if they would surrender, they should be saved. They yielded, eleven of them, and two killed. Not long after, the Wetzel hunting party arrived. Miller had gone down the bottom to kill some game, while the Wetzels floated slowly down under the willows, when a party of thirty Indians there, packing away flour, fired on the Wetzel boat and shot George Wetzel through the body, while he was steering.

He called to his father and brother to lie down, and he would take the canoe out of danger, as he was a dead man anyhow. He paddled over the stream, died about sundown. They buried him on a small island known as Wetzel's Island, one of the Long Reach islands. Miller, hearing the firing, crept up in the tall weeds, and while the others were firing at the boat crossing the river, he fired and killed one and made his own escape by land to Wheeling. The Wetzels also reached there.

[The date given throughout for the death of George Wetzel disagrees with all other accounts, which make it 1786. -- J.C.L.]

### THE DEATH OF JOHN WETZEL, SENIOR

The old man, Lewis Wetzel, and Miller, went down the river on a hunt. Lewis was on shore under the hill, shaking with the ague, some distance below the Muskingum. As old John Wetzel and Miller were paddling along, some Indians on the other side shot into the canoe and shot old Wetzel dead. Miller jumped out, swam over the river, and escaped to Wheeling. As soon as Lewis Wetzel heard the report of the guns, [he] ran, [and] found the tin cup on the shore which he knew belonged to the canoe.

Not seeing the canoe (which the indians had quickly taken away to aid them in swimming over the river), he thought his father and Miller had been captured; and he soon discovered where the horses had stamped, etc. Lewis swam the Ohio with his rifle over his shoulder, and covered it dry, and went nine miles on the trail, and then from his weakened condition from the ague, returned to the river, and went a mile below the Belleville Station. Next day, with a party, Lewis found his father's body in the river, and buried it near the river bank, and subsequently Martin, Lewis, and Jacob paled it in.

Miller was a good hunter, a small man, and was much with the Wetzels. [It is] not known what became of him.

### THE POES

Their famous fight was October 31st, 1782. Seven Wyandottes, and three of them the Half King's sons. It was a very favorable fall -- no frost. Two families of the name of Jackson and two other families left Burgett's Fort, built for the protection of a mill, and went some three miles south. Philip Jackson took his gun and went out to his cabin, a mile and a half distant from the other families, and was captured and his cabin plundered. This was early in the morning (October 30th), and [he] was to have been [back] by breakfast. Not returning, two men went to see what had become of him. They returned with the intelligence of the plundered cabin, etc.

Captain Andrew Poe, who commanded the militia, and his brother Adam, raised a party -- thirteen men altogether. Andrew Poe was a very large athletic man. It was now late in the afternoon. Captain Poe said it would be useless to go to the cabin, and advised that they go direct to [the] river and try and intercept the Indians. All mounted and rode on. That night [they] came to a deserted cabin and found a crib of corn, from which they fed their horses.

Fortunately that night [there] fell a very heavy white frost, the first heavy one to nip vegetation. By day light Poe's party were again in pursuit and struck the Indian trail, where they had gone that morning, as was plainly visible in the frost.

At the mouth of Tomlinson's Run the Indians were discovered making a raft with which to cross the Ohio. One Indian was watching Jackson and keeping sentry, but both keeper and prisoner were intently watching the raft makers, and thus the whites rode up within 25 yards before they were observed. One Indian now made a tomahawk blow at Jackson's head. He dodged and was cut on the shoulder. Before the Indian had time to repeat the blow, one of Poe's men shot him. The Indians now shot Thomas Cherry; then four broke -- two ran up the creek, two down the river, and two remained on the spot. These fugitives were pursued by the men.

The two that stood their ground were the two youngest of the Half King's sons. Captain Poe, seeing them, jumped down the river bank some fifteen feet at a single leap, and struck between the two brothers, and seized them both. The Indians were about the same size, 5 feet 10 inches and 160 pounds weight. Poe got them both down but could not hold them down. One managed to slip out and aimed a tomahawk blow at Poe's head, which he parried off with his left hand, and his wrist [was] half severed -- from this he never fully recovered. At this juncture, while the Indian who had just struck Captain Poe was standing on the beach, Adam Poe came running up with his gun empty, and immediately commenced loading, and the Indian, whose gun was also empty likewise commenced loading, and the strife was who should first get loaded -- the Indian in his haste dropped his ramrod, and thus Adam got a slight advantage, and shot his antagonist dead.

Captain Poe and the Indian in their prostrate scuffle had, the while, rolled into the river, and Andrew finally drowned him and he sunk. Before Andrew got out of the water, two of his own men came dashing up, and mistaking him for an Indian discharged their guns at him -- one of the balls glancing on the water just before him, the other wounding him in the shoulder. Andrew before this accident was nearly exhausted, and in swimming [the] water, and now disabled in one of his shoulders. The timely aid of his brother Adam, who swam in and brought him ashore, probably saved him.

The oldest of the Half King's sons was the commander of the Indian party -- his name was Scotash. He had taken down the river with another Indian, and two others ran up the creek. All save Scotash were killed. He was badly wounded in the hand, but swam across the river and found the dead body of his brother, whom Adam Poe had shot on the shore, and buried him nearby where a tree had upturned the earth. The Indian whom Andrew killed was not named Big Foot, nor was he a particularly large Indian. The track of an Indian had been seen in the country which upon measurement was found to be 13 inches long -- but he was not the victim of Captain Poe.

The Poes were then bachelors -- stout athletic Dutchmen -- lived in a cabin by themselves. Andrew was dark featured -- dark hair and eyes -- could easily carry a quarter cut for four green rails a hundred yards. He was six feet two inches, raw boned, and would weigh 225 pounds -- in his old age considerably exceeded 300 pounds. He died, not many years since, near Beavertown, Pennsylvania.

Adam Poe was of less size than his brother -- 5 feet 10 inches -- strong and heavy. He is supposed to be still living [1845] near Burgettstown, Washington County, Pennsylvania.

## OTHER FRONTIERSMEN: NED SHERLOCK

Edward Sherlock, and thirteen others, at Fort McIntosh (where Beaver now is) in 1780 or 1781, [at the] first snow fall, and were out cutting wood a mile from the fort, and snow falling fast. All were captured and taken to Detroit. Brady was then stationed there. Sherlock was bold and impudent and did not much relish his fare, and would often bawl out, "What a fine fellow George Washington is to what you are!"

The winter of 1782-1783, there were a large number of prisoners at Detroit, and these were quartered on an island in the river near Detroit, Thomas Edgington among them, with a guard. [They] repaired some old cabins, and wood was scarce. Sherlock was set to shoveling [a] snow path. He spoke to the British officer, "Bugger and damn your eyes, do you think one of George Washington's boys is going to be a lackey for you?" Others also refused. Then the officer concluded to scare them, and got a rope, pretending to hang them; he commenced with Sherlock, with [the] rope adjusted around his neck, and bid [him] say his prayers before swinging him off.

"All the prayers I have to say are, "Your maker may roast you on the gridirons of Hell for all eternity -- Hurra for George Washington!" The officer hung him three times, and well nigh succeeded in good earnest, and with difficulty brought him to. Thirteen were thus punished by counterfeit hanging.

Sherlock -- an Irishman -- subsequently returned to Fort McIntosh -- was out on Wayne's Campaign as a drill officer, and was twenty years since [1825] living at Chillicothe. He served through the whole Revolutionary War -- just came to the country when it broke out.

## OTHER FRONTIERSMEN: FITCH, STEVENSON, WILLIAMSON

John Fitch was taken above Marietta, taking the meanderings of the river to make a map, and was sent to Detroit, then to Quebec, and thence to New York, and encountered a fearful storm on the route.

My informant is positive that this was in 1783, as his father was one of the prisoners thus returned, and Thomas Edgington, John Fitch, Daniel Kinney, were among the prisoners confined on the island. Much respect was shown Fitch. Fitch was a prisoner a year or two.

George Stevenson was captured and Spriggs's negro. [This] was about 1780, near Spriggs's Station, now West Liberty.

Col. David Williamson was fully thirty when he went on the campaign -- well respected, [frequently] out on scouts. About 80 or 100 men against the Moravian Town. Robert Wallace had his wife and two children killed.

## SIMON GIRTY

Girty was taken a prisoner when a boy, and raised at Upper Sandusky. Around Fort Pitt Girty was employed as a spy over the Ohio, sometimes one of the pet Indians with him, at a dollar a day. Finally they concluded his spying did not any good, discharged him without the means of paying his back dues. He now asked for a Captain's commission. This was of course refused, he being a drunken and unfit person. He now got James and George [Girty] to join him and report to Sandusky.

Girty's first wife was a fair halfbreed: afterwards he got a Canadian white woman and put away the other. The first wife -- her father lived in the Montour's Creek settlement, and Girty expressed once to her that he would like if he could bring his scalp to her! Thinks Girty was not so bad as represented. Middle size -- well built -- drew pay as interpreter.

## JOHN BINGAMAN

John Bingaman, a brave Dutchman and good hunter and gunsman, lived somewhere between George Edgington's and the North Branch of Potomac; a cabin, wife, and four children. Had a Dutch girl [and] a Dutchman living with them. Early one morning a party of six Indians came before sun rise, and tried to get in at the door. Bingaman and his people were not yet up. An Indian reached in through a crack and cut the string fastening the door, and it opened, and [he] shot into the bed at Bingaman, without hitting him, but slightly wounding Mrs. Bingaman, when Mrs. Bingaman seized his gun and killed him. And the [second] came and Bingaman struck him over the head with his gunpouch and killed him. The third came with a tomahawk and they had a scuffle, the Indian having dropped the tomahawk and both scuffled for it. When a fourth came with a tomahawk, and the girl jumped out of bed and jumped upon this Indian's back and felled him to the floor and held him there.

Bingaman finally got the tomahawk and despatched his Indian, and then finished the one the girl had down. The other two now alarmed, put off, when Bingaman picked up one of the guns belonging to one of the slain [Indians], and shot at a hundred yards and killed another -- thus leaving but one to tell the story. For this good service Bingaman was made a Captain, and was at Fort Pitt with his company, probably with General Forbes.

## CAPTAIN SAMUEL BRADY

In the summer of 1781 [August 1780 -- L.C.D.], a party of over twenty Indians committed mischief on Montour's Run (six miles below Pittsburgh, where Slover was taken). They had their canoe near the mouth of Little Beaver on the south side of the Ohio, covered with brush, under a hill. This was discovered by a man who gave notice at Fort McIntosh. Captain Brady took twenty men, and this man for guide, and marched and took post on the north shore of the Ohio and laid in wait for the Indians -- at length the Indians appeared, loaded with plunder. Brady ordered his men not to shoot till the Indians touched the northern shore.

Seven Indians started in the canoe, while the balance, some fourteen or fifteen, made a raft. The canoe was [some] distance in advance of the raft. When the canoe was within thirty yards of shore a cowardly fellow jumped and ran off for Fort McIntosh, seeing whom the Indians put back, but Brady and his men killed them all. The raft party re-landed on the southern shore, and one of the Indians slapped his posterior, when one Rankin shot off-hand and broke the Indian's back, and [he] died on the spot.

One of the Indians killed in the canoe floated down and lodged on Brown's Island, opposite Holliday's Cove Fort. My informant, then a boy, got the skull, and an ingenious mechanic got the finger bones, and proposed making knife and fork handles of them, which his wife vetoed. [This affair was August 17, 1780 -- L.C.D.]

In 1781, both Captains Brady and Biggs were stationed at Fort McIntosh. [I] don't think Brady was at Fort Laurens. He never did jump the Cuyahoga. He was nearly six feet, very spry and active.

Shortly after the canoe affair -- a few days -- Brady and his party were pursuing Indians who had been doing mischief, and when high up the Alleghany, [they] discovered the enemy some 200 yards ahead, slowly ascending a hill slope, when the same cowardly fellow who had done the mischief before, now shot off his gun, evidently to give notice to the Indians to escape, lest he should have to fight. The Indians fled and escaped, greatly to Brady's chagrin -- it had been his intention to have dogged them along till they camped, and then surrounded and attacked them [the] next morning.

The fellow, on the return of Brady to Fort McIntosh, was cashiered as a coward, and drummed out of the fort.

In [the] summer of 1781, [Brady] commanded Holliday's Cove Fort, his company of 50. This was shortly after the canoe load of Indians were killed. No incident occurred while [they were] there, except that Captain Van Swearingen once visited the fort, and remarked that he had sent his daughter to Philadelphia to get some of the ashes off, and she would be ready for some of the youngsters one of these days. Brady jokingly remarked he would claim her. She was gone a year or two, and when [she] returned, Brady courted and made engaged her -- then went to Kentucky, to Louisville, and [was] gone a year. When he returned, he had his servant -- found his intended engaged to David Bradford -- got back on Sunday, and the next Thursday was the day set for the marriage.

Brady approaches Captain Swearingen, and asks his consent. He replies, "The rascal, who stacked my rye there, put the butts in and the head out, and it [will] have to be done over again." Again Brady would remind him, and he would make the same reply. The stacking was poorly done. Finally Brady, getting warm, said "Captain Swearingen, I am serious. By God, she is mine with your consent or without it, but I would thank you for an answer of some sort." "I would thank you to take her," said Captain Swearingen.

At Pittsburgh were several pet Indians. Brady once rebuked a savage Indian killer -- "I have lost a kind father and affectionate brother at their hands, and I have not went farther in search of revenge than any man had gone, as far as any man could go, or any man dare go, but [I] would scorn to kill an Indian in time of peace, nor women and children in time of war or peace." This my informant heard him say, when stationed at his father's (Thomas Edgington's) at Holliday's Cove Fort in 1781.

Mrs. Brady was educated, and a most worthy and excellent lady -- the belle of her day. Bradford was the best lawyer (until James Ross came out) in the western region, had fame and wealth when he pressed his suit upon Miss Swearingen. Bradford was raised in the region of Carlisle, and was there educated -- got it by promising to become a preacher.

In fall of 1793, Brady had Thomas Edgington as his companion in spying, and while performing their scouts, [they] killed 100 deer that autumn. He was a gentlemanly man, about 6 feet, straight, etc. He was gone to Philadelphia 18 months.

Captain Brady made two trips to Sandusky. On the first trip, Brady and two men hid in some brush, and witnessed the Indians run their horses, doubled the successful one. Two squaws came gathering strawberries near Brady and his companions. These they captured and put off. On return, crossing the Tuscarawas on a raft, they met with a mishap and lost their paddle overboard. Brady had a single load in his rifle, went to kill a deer; [he] saw an Indian party approaching, shot the Indian with a boy tied to him.

Brady then went up to get the Indian's powderhorn, but before he could get it off, the Indians who at first ran off down the hill, he now discovered treed and stealing upon him, and he had to put off, without having had time to get even the much coveted horn of powder. The boy was some eight years old. The two men behind, hearing the firing, ran off, and the squaws escaped. Brady at the crossing of Big Beaver saw the same Indians, and could have had a good shot if he had only had ammunition, which he regretted.

[See Heckewelder's Narrative, p. 281, showing it must have been early in September the fight happened. -- L.C.D.]

In probably 1793, or after, Captain Brady, John Williamson, and Alex Mitchell, and three or four others went out and found an Indian camp of two Indians hunting and trapping on the headwaters of Cuyahoga, and in stealing upon the camp near day light, the Indian dogs, four or five of them, kept an alarm. Brady designated Mitchell and Williamson each to shoot an Indian, and at the signal they fired, but by some misunderstanding they both shot at the same Indian. He bounded up, his heels several feet in the air, and fell dead. The other Indian escaped. Brady brought home a trap he found there -- some of the others also got traps.

John Wetzel was once with Brady to Sandusky and used to say that the plains were excessively hot. [1792 -- L.C.D.]

## BLOCKHOUSE ATTACKS

Opposite Wheeling Island, [was] Lt. Joseph Biggs, with twenty men. [They] were engaged in building a new blockhouse, and made quarters in a vacant cabin; were attacked [in] it in the night. Indians threw flax on fire on the roof and around. This was in the spring of 1791, the same year that Van Buskirk was killed. The dry flax was in a corn crib close by.

There were a chain of blockhouses on the western bank of the Ohio. Next above the Wheeling blockhouse was one a mile below Wellsburg, and

Lieutenant Lawrence Van Buskirk commanded -- my informant one of the soldiers. The next was Yellow Creek blockhouse, 16 miles above what is [now] Steubenville. Captain Forbes had a Pennsylvania company stationed [there], shortly before Van Buskirk was killed. One night Indians stole up, and got in between the sentinel and the blockhouse. He ran for the river, was overtaken and killed. One Indian ran into the blockhouse at the first onset and tomahawked a man, and another was shot while climbing up into the second storey, where the men all placed themselves. The Indians soon decamped.

## MCMAHON'S SCOUT

Major William McMahon (perhaps in [the] fall of 1792) went on a scout of some 60 men; when they reached where Zanesville now is, some of the men were left with horses and provisions -- and two scouts were sent out, McMahon leading one up Owl Creek, and Thomas Edgington (the father of my informant) headed the other. McMahon discovered a camp on Owl Creek, killed two Indians, and Alex. Mitchell wounded another, who escaped -- It was subsequently ascertained from the Indians that this wounded Indian died that afternoon.

The Indians were camped -- four of them on [the] outer bank of the stream on a drizzly rainy night, and the Indians quite merry: Next morning after the Indians were up, laughing and mocking birds, Hezekiah Bukey, William Morrison, and Alex. Mitchell and probably others crept up -- an Indian walked out to the tree behind which Morrison was posted, and the Indian peeping around, M. shot him dead. Bukey shot another, and he fell in the creek; Mitchell shot a third -- he escaped. The other got off.

The two scalps were taken to Wayne's camp at Legionville, and this got McMahon his appointment of Major. He was a brave soldier -- an early settler. He was when killed (both foolishly and foolhardily) about 40 years old -- middle sized. Lived about a mile below Steubenville on a fine bottom of good land on the Virginia side, and subsequently lived on the hill just above Wellsburg. He was cheated out of his fine bottom, having sold it to an emigrant for Continental paper when it was depreciated, but McMahon did not then know it, and lost his place.

## MCCULLOCH'S SCOUT

Captain John McCulloch and Lieutenant Joseph Biggs with a scout of 60 men went to where Zanesville now is -- there selected 37 of the best and went -- followed a horse track and went within hearing of the bells: Captain

McCulloch desired someone to go and report the strength of the enemy. Jacob Wetzel was lame, having had a tree fallen across his legs coming out -- but went, [with] Solomon Hedge and another -- Wetzel crept up and discovered a markee [?] and a number of horses -- thought there were seven or eight persons. He then scoured about [and] discovered another camp below. [He] thus reported.

McCulloch divided the men. He led one party against the unknown camp, and Biggs led the other. At daybreak a squaw with a child came out of the camp where Captain McCulloch was, and approaching a tree behind which John Kimberley was posted, Kimberley shot and killed the mother and child. An Indian boy then ran out, and Captain McCulloch shot at [him] but missed. He escaped. In camp was only an old Indian and a squaw and her three children. These secured, McCulloch, as had been agreed, went to the assistance of Biggs, and met Biggs and his men on the flight, Biggs saying he had seen 40 Indians in camp and doubted not that there were 200. It was no[w] thought advisable to make haste for the main camp on Muskingum, leaving their blankets and provisions where they had lain for the night. Alex Mitchell, who had charge of the prisoners, was directed to kill them. This Mitchell absolutely declined doing, and told the squaw to put off, and she did, and escaped.

John Sutherland, Solomon Hedge, and James Watson lay at the camp, watching, waiting for Biggs to open the fire on the camp -- after daylight two old Indians walked out of camp; one of the men fired and wounded a female, the ball passing through her wrist and slightly wounding her in the breast. She fled to the woods. One of the others fired, and broke the thigh of one of the Indians. Old Isaac Zane, for such he proved to be, now cried out for quarters and told who he was -- that it was his daughter who was wounded. Three men now went into the camp -- sent two of Zane's sons and Sutherland went in pursuit of the wounded girl, and Sutherland mistrusted that they designed killing him, and returned. There were more Indians out hunting, but [this was] not yet known. This was on one of the head branches of Owl Creek.

Wetzel protested against McCulloch's retreat, declaring Biggs's report of Indians was untrue, and it was unfeeling to leave the three men behind. The three men overtook McCulloch at the camp on Muskingum. Biggs was now arrested and both he and McCulloch were tried at West Liberty. Biggs was broke, and McCulloch was suspended four months.

After returning to the camp on Muskingum, seven went by themselves -- Linn, Tom Biggs, and others went to the Indian camp and each got a horse (the Zane camp), and put off and reached Stillwater, and there encamped, were attacked, part killed -- a snow fell the afternoon before camping, and thus the Indians were enabled easily to follow them.

[See Withers, *Chronicles*, p. 308, Mrs. Dinneen Bukey's notes -- L.C.D.]

## VAN BUSKIRK KILLED

[He] thinks it was about the 10th [of] May. George Cox and James Williams discovered signs of indians on Indian Cross Creek, and reported the same night at the blockhouse below Wellsburg, commanded by Lieutenant Lawrence Van Buskirk. Volunteers now were called for to meet at the old Mingo Town next morning at sun rise -- 27 met, my informant and Hugh Brady were along -- the first affair in which Brady aided. Pursued up Indian Cross Creek about a mile, and found but few signs, not indicating more than half a dozen Indians. The Indians had waylaid the path, and thrown some trinkets in it to attract attention, but the men were scattered, and a small portion accidentally discovered the Indians, who had left their ambuscade and posted themselves behind the steep bank of a run.

Isaac Edgington first discovered them and called to the others to tree. The firing now commenced. Van Buskirk exposed himself and crept up towards where the Indians were, and was shot dead by a whole volley of guns. The other whites, attracted by the firing, came up and took part. David Eddy, like Van Buskirk, endeavored openly to creep up towards the Indians, and was shot through the hip with one ball -- another slightly cut the flesh along [?] his ribs, and another ball knocked off the knuckle of his forefinger and shivered his gunstock to pieces, and rent his gun barrel and destroyed his powderhorn -- yet he survived and was able to walk home.

William Rickards was shot across his back and cut near the elbow; and [it] was several months before he recovered. And David Davis was slightly wounded. Some of the men raised the yell, my informant among them, and this was answered by the others, and the Indians instantly fled. They were pursued a little distance. Two of the Indians were mortally wounded, and died that night. The Indians had secreted their budgets under the shelving or hollow bank of the run, and [they] were found, 26 in number -- got one gun.

The plunder was sold for $200 -- new shirts, knives, razors, a spring lancet [?], etc.

## THE BEAVER BLOCKHOUSE AFFAIR -- 1791

A treaty had been held at Pittsburgh, or somewhere along the border, and the Indians would get goods, and by degrees break out again. Some of the Pittsburgh traders built a blockhouse for carrying on the Indian trade, at the mouth of Beaver, and there kept clothes, ammunition, and whiskey. A party of Indians killed Mrs. Lawrence Van Buskirk while [she was] riding to a neighbor's to get some weaving done, on the ridge three miles from Wellsburg towards West Liberty. Six Indians gave her chase. She turned off the path, and in ascending a hill, its steepness so impeded her flight that she [was] overtaken and captured.

That night John Miller and five others waylaid the trail, two miles from where Mrs. Van Buskirk was taken, thinking to intercept the Indians, and in the night, as they lay securely posted behind a log, the Indians came along with their prisoner. Miller and his men, panic struck, broke and ran, and the Indians, alarmed, tomahawked their prisoner.

The next morning, while the party of Indians were on the southern bank of the Ohio, opposite where Steubenville now is, engaged in making a raft, one Jacob Colvin, a traveller from Kentucky, who the night before had tarried at Thomas Edgington's, the Indians saw him and treed, and one did not, a real Big Foot whose track was 13 inches. His aim was to capture Colvin. Colvin, on horseback and finding himself closely beset, levelled his rifle at the pursuing Big Foot. His gun snapped, and then the big Indian jumped to catch him, and into the range of the fire of the other three, who were treed. [They] fired simultaneously, and their brother warrior received their several balls, and dropped dead. Colvin put spurs to his horse and escaped. The next day a party went out from Edgington's and found a dead Indian. This Indian party that killed Mrs. Van Buskirk and attacked Colvin were believed to have come direct from Beaver Blockhouse to the frontier -- such was the sign, and such the relief among the people.

Soon after these events, Captain Brady returned from a scout, and reported that there was a large Indian party hunting on Stillwater. [He] raised a party of men, went, and could find no Indians. It was now proposed to return by way of Beaver Blockhouse, and if any Indians were found there, to kill them. It was put to vote, Brady heading the party who proposed returning via Beaver, and Captain Thomas Patterson, afterwards General Patterson, of West Pennsylvania, the other. They divided equal, and Patterson and his party went down the river, crossed, and returned home.

Brady, Francis McGuire, and their party went to the blockhouse. Thomas Wells and another went ahead a short distance to see. They discovered two young Indians, nearly grown, climbing trees. These discovered the whites and made their escape. The Indian Camp altogether numbered ten Indians, the two young fellows, and two squaws. At the first alarm both of the squaws ran off, but one soon came back and surrendered herself. Joseph Edgington shot her, for which Captain Brady blamed him, [who] thought it unkind and discreditable to make war upon women.

Someone volunteered the remark that Edgington when he shot supposed he was shooting a warrior. The thing dropped, that being deemed a good excuse. This was after the affair or attack was over, but Edgington privately declared he would kill any and every thing in the shape of an Indian whenever he could get a chance, from the size of his fist to an old greyheaded Indian, be they he or she.

Joseph Biggs, Tom Wells, and William Sherrod each killed an Indian, Sherrod chasing his over a mile before he killed him. An Indian ran from camp some distance, and unseen had hid in some drift wood, and snapped his gun at McGuire. Some of the others killed him. Eight warriors were killed, and one squaw.

Lewis Wetzel was along. He having worn out his moccasins, Major McGuire had given him a pair of shoes he had along. McGuire was a very large man, Wetzel but of a middle size -- 5 feet 10 inches -- straight, active, and never wearied in running. Wetzel, in order to keep the shoes on, being much too large for him, tied them as closely as he could, and thus fixed took part in the attack. He and James Campbell pursued two Indians. Campbell, ahead, shot one and broke his thigh. Wetzel some [?] passed this fellow floundering about, soon overtook and killed the other.

This attack occurred in the fore part of the day. Major William Griffith and Thomas Madden took care of the horses, while the others attacked the camp. It was thought the Indians were somewhat in liquor -- else more of them would probably have escaped. Patterson and his party went to Wheeling, crossed, and went to Pennsylvania -- Washington County.

The Proclamation of Governor Mifflin greatly incensed the people, and a meeting was held at Wells's Mills on Cross Creek, and a reward of £50 was offered (raised by subscription) for the first Indian killed -- £30 for the second, £20 for the third, and so on down.

## THE CROW FAMILY

Peter Crow's father and mother and a sister grown and several smaller children were killed on Wheeling. The girl was tomahawked and scalped -- lived four days and died. Peter Crow was absent -- he with Jacob Wetzel and Alexander Mitchell went and crossed the Muskingum, discovered an Indian camp with two Indians -- they surrendered and [were] watched, but somehow one of the Indians went off unnoticed -- probably to some other camp not far distant. The whites crept up to the camp, and Wetzel and Mitchell shot the Indian as he lay asleep in his camp, while Crow shot a pile of blankets on the other side of the fire, thinking possibly it might be the other Indian. Took the scalp and got the first reward -- this was about 1792.

[This was probably in May or June 1791, shortly after the reward offered for scalps. See extract from *Maryland Journal*, 1791, p. 3. -- L.C.D.]

## THE JOHNSON BOYS

The Johnsons, Henry and John, 13 and 11 years, went out to hunt cows, and while cracking hickory nuts, were approached by two Indians whom they took to be their father and uncle. They were captured. The evening being cool, a fire was made. The boys being small were not tied. In [the] night the boys got up, and said [we] must kill the Indians before starting. The older got one of the Indians' guns, and placed [it] across a chunk, aimed at the head of one of the Indians, and his younger brother placed to pull the trigger when he gave the signal; the elder with a tomahawk commenced on his, repeating the blow, the Indian at the first blow flopping into the fire. The younger shot into the jaws of the Indian. By daylight the next morning the boys reached home, found the people gathered.

Jacob Wetzel and a party went out -- found one dead Indian. The shot one had gone off half a mile, but he escaped. His remains were found some time after, twenty miles distant.

# PETER HENRY'S ACCOUNT

### LETTER OF ROBERT ORR TO LYMAN COPELAND DRAPER, FEBRUARY 7, 1851

I have called on Mr. Peter Henry of Butler County, who lives about six miles from the Town of Butler. I was two nights in Butler. It was court week and in inquiring for and about the old man of several of his neighbours and several in town, and all spoke highly of him as an honest good citizen and well respected in that place and that whatever his testament or statement would be that I might rely on it being true -- I was well pleased to hear of him bearing a good character. So I got a horse and rode out there to his house and inquired for him and was told that he was out with the gun round the fields, which I was a little surprised at a man of his age to be out hunting. However, he came in after some time and I found him to be a hearty hale cheerful old man with more intelligence than I had expected to find. He had been some time ago Constable for a number of years, and was a tolerable English as well as German scholar. He showed me his book history that he had.

I told him my business with him. He was very willing and ready to give me, he said, a full statement of all he knew on the subject, and with patience and good humour he gave me a particular account that I think is interesting, which you will find herewith enclosed.

I found that Mr. Henry had an excellent recollection and was very careful and cautious in all his statements to me, and I believe he told me nothing but what he believed to be true, and that parts he had from others was from men he knew and thought they told him the truth in what they stated to him.

I told Mr. Henry that I expected a portion of it would be published. He said that if a history of the Indian difficulties on the frontier would be published in his lifetime, he would have a copy of it for sure.

The old man at one time was said to be a good marksman, and even now he says he can bring a quail down from a tree, as old as he is. The old man was very glad to see me, and was quite pleased to think that the account of him and his sister being taken prisoner and rescued [?] would be published. The old man owns a fine farm there and plenty of everything about him, about six miles southeast of the Town of Butler.

I intended to have called on Mr. Henry sooner, but having no business of my own there, I put it off until now, which I hope will reach you in time.

There are several inquiries that you wish to be informed of that I can give you, but wishe[d] to be better informed myself as to the distances from Mahoning to Red Bank and Brady's Bend by water and by land. The exact distance I cannot now state but will inquire of someone that knows when I am up at Kittanning, where I intend to go to next week and be there until the last week in March. You wish to know something more from Col. Walker.

I gave you a notice of Captain John Craig's death and I told you about the time that Ezekiel Lewis died. Daniel Murphy is yet living.

As to the time [of] Col. Pomeroy's death and Major Wilson's, I will write to you again. I told James Guthrie, son of Alexander Guthrie whose statement I sent you that he should answer your letter that you had written to his father. He said he would do it. The old man, Alexander Guthrie, is dead.

John Sloan, son of Captain John Sloan who defended a station down the river that you gave some account of has told me of some additional evidence that he could give and said he would write it all out and send it to me, which I will forward to you as soon as I get it, and of Richard Wallis, name of Fort, etc., I will write you again from Kittanning, as I will be in Armstrong County until about the last week in March. Next March court there is the third week of March, when I likely will see Col. Walker.

Anything that you wish of me please direct to Kittanning, Armstrong County. After that, please direct to Alleghany City, as I get my letters there -- Alleghany City Post Office now -- not at Pittsburgh Post Office as formerly. Direct under cover to John S. Olney, Rep., Member of Assembly.

You inquire about John or Jack Guthrie. I think you will find there was no such man as John Guthrie. I expect it was Jack that was out with Col. Lochry that you are inquiring after. If I see any old folks from Greensburg, I will inquire.

## PETER HENRY'S ANSWERS TO LYMAN DRAPER'S QUESTIONS

No. 1 -- I was born in Northampton County and of German descent. My father and family moved from that to Westmoreland County about the time that our independence was declared and settled in Hempfield Township about five miles from Greensburg.

No. 2 -- There were nine Indians came to my father's house, but I do not know what any of their names were, or the tribe they belonged to.

No. 3 -- They murdered my mother and three children at the house and one little sister after we had left the house about half a mile.

No. 4 -- It was in the morning just after breakfast. The Indians was at the door before we seen them. The dog barked and I went to the door with the child in my arms, and as soon as I came out one Indian took hold of me and another pulled the child from me and took it by the legs and knocked out its brains against the wall, and went into the house and killed my mother and two other little children, and after taking all out of the house that they wanted to carry with them, and they stripping all the clothes off my mother and [the] children they killed, they then drew the dead bodies out of the house, and set it on fire, and it was burnt.

No. 5 -- My father had gone to mill -- Perry's Mill on Sewickley -- he had gone that morning early. I had no brother Henry.

No. 6 -- I cannot recollect what my age was at that time, but I must have been about ten or perhaps eleven. My sister was about two years younger than me. I think it was before the burning of Hannastown [1782], but am not certain. I was with the Indians about five or six days before rescue.

No. 7 -- The first night we were taken prisoners, the Indians stole seven horses, and the one they got at my father's made eight. That enabled them all to ride but one, and after dividing the plunder, a portion on each horse, they mounted and took my sister and me on horse back with them. The last day we were with the Indians, they killed a bear and two deers, and brought the meat of them to the mouth of Mahoning, where we encamped.

No. 8 -- We crossed the Kiskiminetas River near where the town of Warren is now, on the Armstrong County side, and took across the country and crossed several small streams and struck Mahoning Creek a short distance above the mouth of the Allegheny River and encamped on the point between the river and the bank. The Indians had a canoe there, but how they intended to go, by land or water, I cannot say.

No. 9 -- We were encamped on the North Part and upper side of Mahoning, just on the point between the river and the bank.

No. 10 -- There were no hallowaing or calling by the Brady party to the Indians. All was still and quiet until about day light. When they fired on the Indians was the first notice they had of their approach.

No. 11 -- One Indian was killed. The others broke past and escaped through the lines of Brady's men, some up the river and some up the bank. All of them or a portion of them must have been badly wounded, as there was a great deal of blood on their trail as far as the men followed. I do not know any of their names.

No. 12 -- The Indian that was shot was the principal leader of that band. I did not hear his name. The friendly Indian that was with Brady wanted me to tomahawk him, as they had killed so many of my father's family, but I refused to do it, and the Indian tomahawked and scalped him. He was a large Indian. When shot, he fell, but did not fall on the fire. He fell on his face.

No. 13 -- There were no stallions there. The horses was taken a short distance up the creek to a small bottom and fettered there.

No. 14 -- I did not understand or hear that Brady came over the creek to view the camp, but I was told that a Mr. Joseph Buck did wade over and seen them, but Brady would not let him take a gun with him for fear he would be tempted to shoot one of them, and the great object of their pursuit would have been defied.

No. 15 -- Neither my sister nor me was tied. We had no knowledge of what the Indians intended to do with us. They treated us while with them as well as we could expect. They shared with us at all times to eat of what they had themselves, and they put moccasins on my sister and me shortly after we were taken.

No. 16 -- The first man that spoke to me at the time we were rescued, that I recollect of, was Joseph Buck. He tossed me on the horse and told me not to be afraid, and that they would take me home again. My sister was quite delighted and pleased, and I endeavoured to show my thankfulness by telling them all I knew of the Indians, their numbers, etc., and where they had the horses fettered.

No. 17 -- None of the Indians I seen or heard of ran into the river. They made their escape into the woods up the river or up the creek. Cornplanter was not one of the party. I never understood that he was.

No. 18 -- There was a friendly Indian with the Brady party. I did not hear his name that I recollect of and I never understood but what he acted well in the engagement. All I seen him do was tomahawking and sculping the Indian that was shot there that morning.

No. 19 -- When we were taken prisoners there were nine Indians in the company, and after we crossed the Kiskiminetas River two of them left us, taking a more eastwardly direction, and we seen nothing more of them.

No. 20 -- All the plunder that Brady and his party got at the Indian camp was taken from my father's, except five or six camp kettles that the Indians had at the mouth of Mahoning, and some clothes of a man that it was said this party of Indians had killed on their way into the settlement at or near Kittanning Fort or Green's Station. They got also what the Indians left -- guns, blankets. The Indians had stole eight horses in all. Three of the horses broke off from them, and there were but five of them there then. One of them had been taken from my father. The Indians also took a gun, beds and bed clothes, and all the clothing in the house, and a web of shirteen, a Bible and prayer book, an auger and handsaw, flour and salt, a frying pan, etc., all which was taken by Brady and his men to Pittsburgh and sold, and the money divided amongst them -- all except my father's Bible and prayer book, which he got back.

When the attack was made and the large Indian shot, the rest was all asleep. I was awake at the time and heard the rustling noise of their crawling up, but could not imagine what it was.

No. 21 -- The night after we were taken prisoners, they stole seven head of horses -- and it was said they killed a man near Kittanning Fort or Green's Station on their way into the settlement.

No. 22 -- My father's farm was on the headwaters of Little Sewickley. There were for a few days after we were taken quite an alarm in that neighbourhood, and they collected together for a short time. No party was made up there to follow the Indians, and they returned in a short time to their farms again.

No. 23 -- I heard the names of some of the party. There was Captain Samuel Brady, Peter Parchment, Joseph Buck, a Mr. Amberson, a Mr. Nicholson. I cannot now recollect any more of their names. The men were said to be twenty-four of them altogether, and I have heard nothing of them for a long time.

No. 24 -- I do not know of any other of Brady's engagements with the Indians, only from hearsay. One of them was related to me by a Mr. Jacob Smith, who was a neighbour of mine and was an enlisted soldier under Brady. He gave me an account of an engagement he had with a party of Indians at a place afterwards called Brady's Bend where they killed forty-four or forty-five Indians.

No. 25 -- I cannot tell the time of the attack on Carnahan's Blockhouse by the Indians or the particulars of it, but I have often heard it spoken of.

No. 26 -- I happened to be travelling in course of my business in that part of Westmoreland County near to Wallis's Fort where Major Wilson's farm was and I fell in company with Major Wilson at his house, and he told me of several excursions and engagements he had after and against the Indians, and said that sometimes the Indians was too many of them [illegible] to run, and other times they chased the Indians. He showed me the place where he had shot an Indian and where he fell. The Indian had shot a Mr. Redick. I was engaged scout by the man when he shot him. I told Major Wilson that I had been a prisoner with them and rescued by Captain Brady, which was the reason, I suppose, that he told me so much about them. He was said to be a very brave and useful man on the frontier and knew well how to use a rifle.

No. 27 -- I have no knowledge of Captain John or Jack Guthrie, nor knew him.

No. 28 -- I cannot say anything about Richard Wallis. Wallis had a mill there, and the fort or blockhouse I understood was built near the mill, and likely took its name from that, and was called Wallis's Fort. It was in Westmoreland County, not far from the Kiskiminetas River.

My age when I was taken prisoner, as well as the short time I was with them, is all and the only apology I have to offer for not being able to answer fully several of the foregoing inquiries. So answers Peter Henry.

## PETER HENRY'S ACCOUNT OF HIS CAPTURE AND OTHER EVENTS

[Peter Henry of Clearfield Township, Butler County, Pennsylvania, gave me the following account of his being taken prisoner by the Indians and of his being rescued by a party that followed them, under the command of Captain Samuel Brady.

Mr. Henry states that he was born in Northampton County and of German descent and that about the year 1778 or 1779 his father with him and the rest of the family moved into Westmoreland County, Hempfield Township, about four miles from Greensburg, Pennsylvania. -- R.O.]

Westmoreland County at this time was on the frontier part of Pennsylvania and the Indians had began for some summers before that of committing depradations of the then frontier settlements of that country, in murdering, burning, stealing their horses and destroying their property and carrying off prisoners, etc., and my father's house and family did not escape their savage cruelty.

It was, I think, in the summer of 1781 or 1782 that a party of nine Indians came to my father's house just after breakfast. The dog barked and I opened the door and the youngest child in my arms, and as soon as I had opened the door an Indian took hold of me and an other pulled the child from me and took it by the legs and knocked its brains out against the wall. The others had rushed into the house, and killed my mother and two other of the youngest children, and took me and my two sisters younger than me prisoners. My father had left home early that morning to Perry's Mill, five miles off.

The Indians before they left the house took everything that they thought was worth taking that they could carry with them, bed, bed clothes, and all kind of clothing that was in the house, a web of shirteen, flour, salt, butter, frying pan, handsaw and auger, a rifle gun, a Bible and prayer book, and a horse of my father's that was in the stable. They stripped the clothes all off my mother and little sisters that they had killed, and took all along. They then drew the dead bodies of my mother and [the] children out of the house and burnt the house.

The Indians put all on the horse that they got at father's that they could get fastened on, just as much as would lie on him, and the rest of their plunder they packed themselves, and was all pretty full ladened when they gathered up all they took with them.

I do not now recollect my age when taken prisoner, but I suspect I was about ten or perhaps eleven years old, my sisters, say, one nine and the other seven years old that was prisoners. We had not gone more than half a mile when my youngest sister who they was leading by the hand continued to cry, calling for her mother, and one of the Indians took out his butcher knife and ran the child entirely through the body that I seen the point of the knife that came out at its back. She sunk down at once. The Indian gave me a slap in the face and motioned for me to go on. My other sister was then crying a little. I told her to quit crying or the Indians would kill her too, and she soon quit. They put moccasins on my sister and me.

They travelled about five or six miles that day, being all heavy ladened, and stopped before night a while, and stole seven horses that night and the one got at my father's was eight. They then the next morning divided their plunder on the horses, so that they all rode but one. They took my sister and me on horse back with them.

When the Indians left my father's, they took a homeward direction, thinking, I suppose, if they could make their escape with what they had got there, they would be doing very well, with a chance of picking up a few horses by the way, which they did, and made the horses pack what they had done the day before. The following night they fettered the horses out to pasture and three of them broke off from them that night. The way the Indians fetter or are fastening them is they hold them back and ties their two forefeet together, say about eighteen or twenty inches apart, so that they can step around slowly so as to gather something to eat.

We went all and crossed the Kiskiminetas River near where the town of Warren is now, in Armstrong County. Two of the Indians left us after we crossed the Kiskiminetas River. They took a more eastwardly course than we done, and I seen nothing more of them.

We took across the country, keeping more north, and keeping Kittanning for some miles on our left, as I afterwards understood, and crossed several small streams, and struck Mahoning Creek a short distance above its mouth and came down to its mouth and encamped there on the upper side of the point between the mouth of Mahoning and the Allegheny River.

The day that we got to the mouth of Mahoning we travelled but a short distance. The Indians killed a bear and two does that day, and they encamped early in the evening. They brought the meat of all to the camp that evening, and some of them was busily engaged in cutting the meat off the bones and drying it on a little rod or stick over the fire to make what the Indians call Jerk -- dried meat to carry with them.

The bones they boiled with flour and salt they got at my father's to make a great supper of soup. One of them was very expert in cooking and turning pan cakes. He had a long-handled pan that they took from my father's and he had the batter mixed up and would pour it into the pan, which was swimming in gravy and grease, as they had plenty of bear meat and fat.

That night this Indian would swing round the cake in the pan -- then he would throw it up and turn the cake out of the pan, and would catch the cake again in the pan and when it would fall back into the pan again, it would make the grease and fat fly all round, which afforded during the cooking operation a great deal of laughing and sport, as the mode of turning the cakes and making the grease fly round was likely new to them. One or two of them was sitting mending their moccasins near the fire, and the cook who suffered the most in the scalding scattered grease from the cook's exploits in turning the pancakes.

Early in the evening the Indians brought a canoe into the mouth of Mahoning, either down the creek or from the river. I did not see it until it was there. They had six or seven small camp kettles in it. I did not hear where they came from.

The day the Indians came to the mouth of Mahoning, they cut several short forks or crutches to fix up something like packsaddles. Having a saw along, they sawed up the sides of an old canoe, and they had something, I suppose, to fasten the sides to the crutches so as to make the packsaddle to lay on the horse's back, with a bag or quilt under it. In this way they intended to carry off all their plunder, with the five horses that they still had there. The horses they took up Mahoning Creek about a quarter or half a mile to a small bottom. There they fettered them. I rode one of the horses up to where they left them.

After supper, when they had their packsaddles made and their work done, but supper with them lasted a long time. They eat a while and quit and begin again, as I suppose it was the richest and most sumptuous supper they had got for a long time, or perhaps ever had in their lifetime.

At a late hour, before they lay down, they had a dance. They danced around one man sitting that made some kind of music for them on a pan. They took hands some times and danced around. They sped and hollowaed at a great rate. They had made a great deal of noise that day in shooting and whooping when they killed the bear and two deers -- they thinking, I suppose, that they were out of danger, little expecting that Captain Brady and twenty-three others was lying across the mouth of Mahoning from them, watching their movements.

I understood that Captain Brady and his men got on our trail where we crossed the Kiskiminetas River, and as we had several horses with us, they could easily follow our trail. The Brady party got up in hearing of us early on the day we got to Mahoning, but they kept back, waiting until we would encamp before they would commence the operations.

The Indians appeared to be in fine spirits, considering, I suppose, that they had made a profitable trip to the frontier settlements, with their prisoners, plunder, and horses, and so far safe on their way home, and as they supposed, out of all danger, little expecting that the morning light would show [that] a reverse of all their flattering anticipations and hopes was awaiting them at the next morn's early dawn.

It was late when the Indians lay down to sleep, thinking themselves secure. They slept sound. One of the Indians who appeared to be the leader and the largest one of them attended particularly that evening and continually throughout the night to drying their meat, making Jerk of it so as to carry it with them.

It was said that one of the Brady's men, by the name of Joseph Buck, waded over Mahoning that night, who likely was sent by Brady, or indeed Brady might have been over himself to view the ground about the encampment, but Brady would not let Buck take his gun with him for fear, as he was a pretty resolute fellow, he might see a good chance of shooting one and do it, which would have given the alarm, and the great object of their pursuit would have been defeated -- and Buck crossed back again, and, I suppose, gave all the information he had, and Brady and his men some time before day went up the creek a piece, where they could wade it, and crossed over and came on down and quietly and cautiously surrounded the Indian camp, some distance off at first; as day light began to make its appearance they would crawl up still a little closer to their camp, and in their closing up occasionally made some noise that was heard by the large Indian that was up and attending to drying the meat, and he walked two or three times a few steps from the fire and listened and would give a little whoop and holloa as if it was to scare off some wild animal, as I believe he thought the cracking of the brush or noise he heard was some wild animal that had smelled their cooking meat.

I was awake lying on the ground and could hear all the little noise they made for some time, but I could not imagine what the noise was. A thought of hope ran in my mind that it might be some of my friends or others that were coming after us, but I lay quiet where my sister and me was lying, until all was over and the Indians fled.

Again this time it was beginning to be light enough to see to shoot and the large Indian preparing the meat in drying. He was the only one of them that was up: the rest was all sound asleep. I was told that the word went round the Brady men that a Mr. Nicholson who was a very sure shot was to shoot the big Indian at the fire, at which time the rest of the Indians would of course jump to their feet, at which time all that had a good chance and a sure mark of not missing was to shoot, but as it was scarcely light enough to see distinctly to be very careful in shooting, for fear they would shoot some of the prisoners, as Brady was not aware but that party of Indians had taken a good many prisoners and was there with them.

So Nicholson at the proper time shot, and down went the big Indian. He was shot through the body just below the arms. I was still awake and saw him reel round, and he fell forward on his face, and kind of raised himself on his hands and feet, but soon sunk down. He moaned and screamed most awfully but soon died. At this time the other Indians had jumped to their feet and was shot at, but they darted off at once and made their way out through the line of the Brady men, some running up the river and some up the creek. One young Indian must have been badly wounded: I seen him jump up and down and he screamed, but he made his way into the woods. None of them ran into the river that I seen or heard of.

It was supposed that if the Brady party had not been afraid of shooting, for fear there were a number of prisoners with them and they might have got up when the Indians rose up, and it not being light enough fully to discern them, which was the cause assigned for not shooting them all, or nearly so -- there were seven Indians there in all: one was killed and six made their escape.

The first man that I recollect of coming to me was Joseph Buck. He tapped me on the head and told me not to be afraid, and that they would take me home again. My sister and me was highly pleased, I assure you, when we found how matters was, and that we would be released and get home again, and in order to show my thankfulness I told them everything I knew about the Indians, what they had done, etc., and told them where the horses was, and said I would go up with them that was going for them, but Brady would not let me go for fear they might be some other Indians lurking about and they might catch me, as I was young. However, some of the men went up for the horses where I directed them where they found find them, and they got the five that was there.

The friendly Indian and some of the other men that was there wanted me to tomahawk the Indian that was shot there that morning, and they said I should do it as that party had murdered so many of my father's family, but I refused to do it, and the friendly Indian then tomahawked and scalped him.

It was the general opinion that morning amongst the men that the six Indians that escaped was all or nearly all wounded, and some of them severely, on account of so much blood being found on their trail, which they [Brady's men -- J.C.L.] had followed for some distance, but they did not come up with any of them. These six Indians ran off almost naked. They had their moccasins off drying by the fire, as they had done generally every night before, and a portion of their other dress was laid off, and barefooted and the next thing to being naked, they had not even time to take their guns or blankets with them, as they were fired at the moment they got to their feet from their sound sleep, and they darted off at once in this situation -- naked and wounded and having no guns with them to kill anything to eat. The most of them likely never reached their home.

I might mention here as evidence of the fate of those Indians that Simeon Hoover and one of my neighbours in Westmoreland County was taken prisoner the summer before I was, and he told me after he returned home that he was taken into the same village or tribe that those nine Indians came from, that same place, and that there was but one of the nine that ever got home, and that he was almost naked and scarcely able to walk when he came home, and he said that this Indian on his return home gave the following account of himself and his camerades on that excursion: that they had made their way into the frontier settlements of the white people and had been pretty fortunate; that they had some prisoners and several horses and a good deal of plunder with them, and they was on their homeward route for some days, and they expected they were safe and out of danger of being pursued, and very unexpectedly to them they were followed and overtaken by Brady and a party of white men that surrounded their camp at night, and at day light fired on them, and one was killed on the ground; the rest made their escape; Brady and his men rushed on them so rapidly that they had not time to get their guns and were forced to fly barefooted and almost naked and having nothing to eat and no guns to kill anything, and several of them being badly wounded that had died of their wounds, and others with fatigue and hunger; and that he had almost despaired of reaching home.

Simeon Hoover said that when this Indian made that report, that he never seen such an uproar amongst them all the time he was with them, in mourning, crying, and lamenting, which was principally confined to the squaws. It was a full day of mourning in that town that day. The men of there was also affected on hearing the news of their fate, and he began to get afraid that some of them would take a notion of vetting their anger and revenge on him, and he went and hid and kept out of the way for a day or two, and he said that his adopted father asked him where he had been; he told him that he had kept out of the way for fear some of the Indians who had their friends killed might out of revenge kill him, but his father told him he need not have been afraid: they would not have injured him. But he was afraid to try them.*

[I have inserted a word here for clarity: "need not *have* been afraid." But I suspect this is in fact an early use of Western Pennsylvania *need* plus participle to indicate conditional necessity, as in "the car *needs* washed" or "the grass *needs* mowed." -- J.C.L.]

* He was afraid to trust them after what he seen them doing at the time he was taken prisoner. -- P.H.

He also said the character of Brady was pretty well known amongst them there, and that they seemed to be more afraid of him than any other one that he had heard them speak of, on the frontier settlement.

I might mention here what a fine breakfast the Brady party had that morning. Bear meat, venison, and Jerk was fine eating as it was well dried in the kettle, and though of the performance of that morning, a portion of the meat had fell into the fire and got burnt, there were still great abundance left. Brady and all the men there with him was dressed and painted just as the Indians were. All wore caps so as to appear as like them as possible, that their appearance would not alarm the Indians until they would get near enough to them to shoot at them.

It was said that when this friendly Indian and Brady was on the trail or in the pursuit of Indians, that the Indian would generally go forward on the trail some distance, so that if he would come on them suddenly, he could talk to them and tell them just what he pleased, and leave them and return to Brady again. It was said that he was a faithful trusty fellow to Brady in all their excursions and engagements they had with them.

Mr. Nicholson and the man that shot the big Indian, and the friendly Indian that was with Brady got a canoe that they said they found hid near the mouth of Mahoning some place, and put all the plunder and baggage that was there then into the canoe, the Indians' guns and all, and took my sister and me into the canoe and went on down the Allegheny River. The horses was taken down by Captain Brady and some of his men. We all met at what they called Kittanning Fort, ten or twelve miles down, about the middle of that same day. They did not remain there long, and went on that afternoon and passed Green's Station and several other blockhouses on the river where men was stationed at, between that and Pittsburgh, where we got to our destination the third morning after we left Mahoning, and we met Brady and his men there again.

All the plunder, horses, etc., that was brought down to Pittsburgh from the Indian camp at Mahoning was sold and the money, as I was told that the articles sold for was divided amongst the Brady party that rescued us, which I think were the men justly entitled to, as I was told the men that were along was neither enlisted nor drafted and of course would get no other pay than that -- of all the property my father lost, nothing was returned to him but his Bible and prayer book.

Nicholson and the friendly Indian worked the canoe down the river quietly and with a great deal of caution, particularly in the morning after we left Mahoning and until we got to Kittanning Fort, and indeed all the way down to Pittsburgh. Whenever they channelled them to the right hand side near the shore, they made my sister and me lie down in the canoe so as not to be seen from the shore. Nicholson was in Indian dress and him and the Indian was both painted so that if they had been seen or hailed by Indians from the shore, the friendly Indian would have spoken to them and passed off as Indians until they would have got out of their reach.

They both said that it was not at all unlikely that they would see or be seen by Indians that might be lurking about on the north east side of the river, on their way going or returning from the frontier settlements. We was stopped at several blockhouses on our way down that there were men stationed at, but seen no Indians on our way to Pittsburgh.

This large Indian that was shot at the Indian camp at the mouth of Mahoning, he had when they took me prisoner a fresh sculp carrying with him, and it was afterwards said that this party had killed a man some place near Kittanning Fort or Green's Station when on their way into the Settlement, and the man that was killed was said to be an officer, and that a part of his clothes was found with this party of Indians, and the clothes was recognized and known to be clothes that this man or officer had on when he was killed, and it was likely his sculp that this big Indian had with him.

I think that one of the nine that took me prisoner must have been a white man and a German scholar, for he frequently, when he had time, was engaged in reading in my father's Bible or prayer book in German, as on other evidence he had a beard amd shaved while I was with them.

OF CAPTAIN SAMUEL BRADY

You ask me if I know any other exploits performed by Mr. Brady in his excursions and engagements with the Indians. I know of no other, only from hearsay, but one account I heard of him. I heard several others, but this one was told to me by a Mr. Jacob Smith, who lived in Westmoreland County, not far from Greensburg. I heard him speak of the engagement often, as Brady was a great favourite of his, and he liked to talk about it. He told me that Captain Brady with a company, and several other companies -- I cannot recollect who he said was the commander, but they were going up the Allegheny River against the Indians. This Jacob Smith was one of Captain Brady's men, an inlisted soldier, and had been under and with Brady frequently.

I cannot recollect what year he said it was, but early in the summer, and during the Indian troubles on the frontier settlements. He said they were going on up the Allegheny River, keeping a lookout for Indians, as they had heard by some means that there were a large party of Indians that had started and was on their way down the river, bound of course for murdering and pillaging our frontier settlers, as Westmoreland County was then a frontier settlement, and on their going up the Allegheny River, on the North East side of the river, several miles above the mouth of a creek called Redbank, we came to a large bottom, where we halted a short time, and he understood that this place was afterwards called Brady's Bottom or Brady's Bend.

We had our spies out in advance of us, who after a short time came back and told us that they had seen a number of Indians coming down the river, and that there were eight canoes and seemed to be all pretty well ladened with them. Then the great matter was to know how to act or what plan to pursue for the best so as to get them decoyed in and induced to land so as to have a good chance at them. Captain Brady, he proposed a plan and said he would take a few men with him and go down on the shore and walk along as if he did not see the Indians, and when the Indians would see them, to appear to be alarmed and run up the bank, and for all the other men to be lying in wait for them if they would land.

So Brady's plan was readily adopted. Brady took five men with him to the river shore, and waited there until the Indians came in sight. They then moved up the shore slowly and searchingly, as if they did not see the Indians. At last the Indians seen them, and immediately wheeled their canoes for the shore towards them. There Brady and his men, as if they had just seen them, appeared to be alarmed and ran up the bank where the rest of the men was lying placed and in wait for them at the place.

Brady came up the bank. The Indians was not long in landing and they ran up the bank with a rush on Brady's trail, and our men was prepared for them, and we opened a pretty heavy and destructive fire on them before they were well aware of any danger. The Indians took trees at once, and kept up the firing for some time, as they seemed unwilling to run, but before long they began to retreat back towards the shore amongst the tall grass, bushes, and driftwood, where they sheltered and defended themselves for a time, not willing to abandon their canoes, but finally was forced to do so. As our men was afraid that a portion of them would endeavour to escape in their canoes, they pressed closely on them, and those that was able was forced to fly, some running one way and some another.

Several of them took into the river and escaped in that way. He did not know how many Indians there were. They had eight canoes they got, and what plunder was in them, which consisted of some blankets, small camp kettles -- pain du lead, provisions, new moccasins, two or three dressed deer skins, and a quantity of strap and cords supposed to have been for the purpose of tying prisoners with leading horses.

After the Indians fled, our men pursued them a short distance as they scattered round, but did not follow them far. We hunted all round to see how many of them we had killed, and we found in all forty-four or forty-five, and likely a number that got off was wounded, as our people had much the advantage of them, all being ready and prepared for them as soon as they would rise on the bank. The Indians, thinking there were only five or six men, ran unguardedly up the bank just where our men wanted them to come -- and was previously notified to be ready to make sure and safe shooting, which from the number killed, a good many of us did not miss their mark.

I have heard a great deal about Brady and many of his exploits and adventures with and amongst the Indians and indeed many of them are extraordinary ones, but this is the only account that I recollect particularly well as I have heard my neighbour Mr. Smith often speak of it, and at all times spoke in the highest terms of Captain Brady and of his quick ready discerning judgment in cases of sudden emergency, and said that Brady should and ought to have all the credit that was gained in the victory and in being so successful in it, as he said it was all done on Brady's plan and his good conduct and management in accomplishing what was so much desired by inducing the Indians to land -- the defeat of this party of Indians was the means no doubt of saving the lives and property of many of the frontier settlers that would in all probability have fallen a prey to their savage cruelty if they had not been in this way prevented.

So ends Jacob Smith's account to me [Peter Henry] of that engagement.

OF MAJOR WILSON

You ask me if I knew anything about Major Wilson. He did not live in my immediate neighbourhood, but in the same county, Westmoreland, but I seen him frequently and have often heard of his courage and bravery the time of the Indian wars, in defending the frontier settlers, and I happened to be at his house either during or about the close of the Indian war, and I was anxious to hear something from him and I told him that I had been taken prisoner and that they had murdered my mother and four of her children, and that I was rescued by Captain Brady and that I had served two terms in the Militia at the frontier blockhouses.

The major then told me of several occurrences that took place in that neighbourhood that I recollect, and I will tell you what he told me of them.

That he had several little brushes, as he called it, with the Indians, sometimes by himself and sometimes in company with some of his neighbours, or some militia men generally stationed at Wallis's Fort on the adjoining farm, and the Indians would sometimes chase them, and sometimes they would chase the Indians. At one time, he said, there was a man shot -- I do not recollect his name -- about one mile from Wallis's Fort, and about twenty-five or thirty of us volunteered to go out and bury him, and the Indians, he supposed, expected some party out from the fort, and they were lying in ambush on each side of the road near where the men lay, and they fired on them, and killed eight or ten of them. The balance then retreated to the fort, and the Indians pursued them closely, firing on the hindmost. Some of the men was clumsy and could not run fast, and would have likely been nearly all or the most of them killed, if it had not been for him and two other active riflemen that would occasionally stop and get behind trees, and would load and fire occasionally back at the Indians, and in this way they kept the Indians back until the other men got to the fort.

He said it was close nicking that day with himself. He said he kept the hindmost of all shooting and keeping the Indians back, and to his great surprise he found he had shot his last load [and] had not any other bullet, and to add to his surprise an Indian had went round a little, and got a bead on him, and he seen him standing on a bridge that he had to cross over, and the Indians was pressing on behind him. He seen his danger and determined to make a desperate effort, and he took hold of his rifle by the barrel end, and drew it up, and ran at the Indian and hollowaed at him for a black villain that he would kill him, and threatening him with loud words, and the Indian before he got to him ran off the bridge. Then he said he ran his best. Several guns cracked and he heard the bullets whistle past him, but none hit him. He was there near the fort, and the Indian gave up the chase. He said the Indian that was before him on the bridge likely had no load in his gun or he would have shot him, unless by his rapid determination and his running at him, and hollowaing about at him, had stupified his courage.

The Major told me that he thought and believed that in this chase the Indians gave them, that he must have killed two Indians that was advancing after them, for he had two fair chances [and] thought he had shot two, as some missed his mark.

Major Wilson told me of several attacks the Indians had made on the farmer's houses when they thought there were but few men in the house, and sometimes they succeeded and sometimes they did not. He said they attacked his neighbour Colonel Pomeroy's house one day and there were none in the house, and his wife ran bullets and loaded for him, and he shot out often and kept up a regular fire. The Indians had sheltered themselves near his house, behind a small building, and shot from that. Pomeroy was upstairs and that floor was laid with loose boards, and him and his wife would run frequently over the boards.

The Indians was near enough to hear the noise, and Pomeroy spoke loud and called over a number of names, and told them to shoot the black rascals down, and that with the noise he made in running over the floor induced the Indians to go off after they had kept up a fire on the house for nearly half a day -- thinking no doubt that there were several in the house. The firing was heard at Wallis's Fort, and a party came out from it, and took him and his family to the fort that night. It was about two miles from there.

Major Wilson told me of another act of his own in killing an Indian. He said at another time when the Indians paid them a visit, that he was out not far from his house, and he seen an Indian chasing a white man, a Mr. Redick, and he ran into the house for his gun, and before he got out and run to where he was, the Indian had shot Redick and was in the act of sculping him, and Wilson shot the Indian, who only ran a few steps and fell dead. He showed me the place where he had shot the Indian -- Major Wilson knowing that I had been a prisoner and so many of my father's family had been murdered by them. This was the reason, I suppose, that he told me so much about them.

They were said to be a brave set of men in my neighbourhood during these Indian troubles -- Col. Pomeroy, Major Cahill, the Wilkeys, and the Guthries. Major Wilson had the reputation of being a brave and useful man in aiding in the defense of the then frontier settlement of that country. I might also state that when I seen the friendly Indian a day or two after him and Mr. Nicholson had brought us down to Pittsburgh -- he was dressed in a splendid manner. He had a large silver plate hanging on his breast suspended by a silver chain around his neck, something like the shape of a half moon -- and silver bands clasped around his arms, and scarlet leggins handsomely trimmed off, which I presume was presented to him by the commanding officers at Pittsburgh for his services.

As soon as my father heard that my sister and me was in Pittsburgh, him and one or two of our neighbours came down for us and took us home. It was about fifteen or sixteen days from the time we were taken prisoner until we got home.

[Mr. Henry also states that his sister Margaret that was taken prisoner with him was twice married and her husbands are both dead and she is yet living in Hempfield Township, Westmoreland County, near Greensburg. -- R.O.]

My sister and me was the only prisoners that that party of Indians had with them -- and they did not tie either of us, thinking, I suppose, that we were too little and young to attempt to run off from them.

My age as well as the short time I was with the Indians is all the apology I have to offer for not being able to answer more fully several of the inquiries you made.

Agreeable to an entry made in the old family Bible belonging to my Father of the ages of the family, I was born on the 16th of June, 1770, which makes me now eighty years of age on the 16th of June last.

OTHER EXPERIENCES

I was drafted in Westmoreland County, to serve a two months tour under Captain John Craig and marched with him to what was called Craig's Blockhouse not far from the Town of Shaloeta on Crooked River in Indiana County. I was not eighteen years of age, wanting two or three weeks, but was willing to go, and I volunteered and went out several times on short excursions with John Mahaffy and John Gordon, who was then employed as spies at that time and under pay to go out and around exploring the frontier settlements and gaining notice of the appearance or signs of the approach of Indians.

While at the blockhouse, a Mr. Miller came there as an express from Kirkpatrick's, a few miles off, that the Indians had attacked Kirkpatrick's house there and had killed two or three of them, and about ten or twelve of us volunteered and went there and found the Indians had killed and wounded some two or three, and one of the Kirkpatricks had shot an Indian that was lying there. John Mahaffy was one of the party that was along with us.

The account given us that morning of the Indians attacking the house was this: that the Indians had crawled up near the house while Mr. Kirkpatrick was going about worship early in the morning. They opened the door, and [went] onto a small porch at the door. The Indians fired at them.

One of the men that was shot fell in the door, and it could not be shut at once, and one of the Indians jumped up on the porch and wanted to force his way into the house, but one of the Kirkpatricks, being a pretty stout active man, took hold of the Indian and threw him off the porch, then drew the dead man into the house and shut the door, and ran upstairs with his rifle, from which place he could see one of the Indians who was standing behind a pig pen in the act of loading his gun, and Kirkpatrick, knowing how to use a rifle, shot the Indian. He ran off a few steps and fell.

The other Indians that was there, when they seen that one was shot, they ran off. When Kirkpatrick shut the door, the Indians shot several balls in or through the door. One of Kirkpatrick's little daughters was wounded, and one or two of the men that were there in the house was killed, and one or two wounded. John Mahaffy and me trailed the Indian that had been shot there that morning up to the door, and Mahaffy sculped him.

I went on with a portion of the men that was there as a guard with the Kirkpatrick family, to what was then called Clark's Mill on Crooked Creek -- now Frantz's Mill -- and returned the next day to Craig's Blockhouse, and at the expiration of the two months I returned home.

[Peter Henry also states he thinks that it was the following summer that he was out with Captain Craig, that he was again drafted to serve a two months tour under Captain Jacob Painter in Westmoreland County, and was marched to what was called Chambers's Blockhouse, near the Kiskiminetas

River, and not far from the Town of Warren -- and states that he was out frequently while there on scouting parties up and down the Kiskiminetas River. -- R.O.]

A small party of us went down the Allegheny River and on to the mouth of Bull Creek on the West Side of the river, where the Town of Tarentum now stands, where there were a company of men stationed, and then we came back again.

At another time a party of us made up from different stations along on the frontier posts took an excursion down the river and went on as far as the mouth of Beaver below Pittsburgh to a station there -- I think it was called Fort McIntosh -- from that we went up Beaver some distance, then struck across to Bull Creek, then down Bull Creek to the mouth at the blockhouse, [and] from that back to our places again. And after the expiration of the two months, I left Chambers's Blockhouse and went home.

[Mr. Peter Henry said this ended what little services he had performed in the War of 1776 and in the Indian War, and that in the War of 1812 he said he volunteered from Butler County and went to Black Rock, but did not do much there -- only got some pullets, bacon, and beef and came home again.

From all I could hear and find out about Mr. Henry, he has been no doubt a pretty resolute brave man, willing at all times to serve his country when required. He owns a fine farm six miles from Butler. He is cheerful and pleasant and everything plenty about him, and is now eighty years of age on the 16th of June last (1850). -- R.O.]

# A BRIEF NARRATIVE

Giving an Account of the Time and Place of Birth of
Captain Spencer Records
His Movings and Settlements
With Incidents That Occurred
Relative to the Wars with the Indians

With a Brief Account of His Father
Josiah Records

Written by him, the said Spencer Records

INTRODUCTORY

I have written the following narrative, partly for my own satisfaction and amusement, and partly for the information of my children, as by it they may become acquainted with some things they would otherwise be ignorant of.

I have written it briefly, stating every thing in as few words as possible; which will take less writing and reading, and will probably be better understood.

October 8th, 1842                                            Spencer Records

Spencer Records, son of Josiah Records and Susan Tully his wife, was born on the 11th day of December 1762, in Sussex County, State of Delaware. My father and mother were both descendants of English ancestors.

I shall in the first place, give a brief account of my father, Josiah Records, which will serve as an introduction to my own. Capt. Josiah Records, son of John Records and Ann Galloway his wife, was born on the first day of May old style in the year 1741 in Sussex County, State of Delaware. In 1765, my father with his family, his mother, sister Susanna and his two brother-in-laws, James Quotermos and James Finch, with others, embarked on board of a sloop in the Nanticoke River, descended it to its mouth in the Chesapeake Bay, thence to the mouth of the Potomac, and up that river to Georgetown, and having landed there, proceeded on to Antetom creek near Hagarstown, and there wintered.

In the spring of 1766, my father and his two brother-in-laws crossed the Alleghany mountains, and took up land near the foot of Laurel Hill, and near Dunbar's creek, so called from the circumstances of Colonel Dunbar having encamped thereon, with the rear of Braddock's army, at the time of his defeat. Braddock was mortally wounded, taken to that camp, there died, and was buried.

That country at that time, was known as the Redstone country, and so called from Redstone creek, which running through a part of that country, entered the Monongahela river, twelve miles northwest of where Uniontown now stands, and near where the town of Brownsville is now built. After clearing ground, planting it in corn, and working it, they returned back, and in the fall moved over the mountains.

My father hired Peter Elot with his cart and three horses to move him, and took my uncle Quotermos's blacksmith tools in the cart, all but the anvil; it was heavy and had to be left. They took Braddock's old road: At that time there were not more than ten or twelve families in that settlement, a few about the broad ford of Youghioghany; some about the stone old fort, and a few about Fort Pitt, perhaps not more than one hundred in all. However, emigrants crossed the mountains rapidly, and settlements were soon extended to a considerable distance in different directions.

Perhaps it may not be amiss, to give a short sketch of the manner in which the first settlers of the Redstone lived. As they had to pack over the mountains on horse-back, they could carry but little more than their clothing, beds, and cooking utensils. As deer, bear, and turkies were plenty, they were supplied with meat by hunting; their cloth was home-made, some dressed deer-skins; many yards of linen were made of nettles: their bread was made by pounding corn in a hommony block. Coffee and tea were not used. At that time there were no store goods west of Laurel Hill; all articles they could not make themselves, were packed over the mountains from Hagerstown, a distance of 130 miles. Some persons made a business of buying bear and deerskins, ginseng, etc., packing them to Hagerstown, and fetching such articles as were needed. My father being a good hunter, and killing a great many deer and bears, made a trip to Hagerstown every winter after hunting time, and got such articles as he stood in need of.

The people there, at that time, lived happier, and better contented, than the people do there at this time, with all the luxuries, fine dress, pride, vanity, pomp and show.

About the year 1768 [1766?], Philip Shoot built a tub-mill on Dunbar's creek. My father did the mill-wright work, and my uncle Quaturmos did the black-smith work. It was built on a very small scale, and very imperfectly, for want of tools. I remember, that my uncle made use of the pole of an axe for an anvil. This mill would grind fifteen bushels of grain in a day, which being sufficient for that neighborhood was a great relief. This was the first mill built west of Laurel Hill. About two years afterwards, Henry Beason built a mill on Redstone creek, and some time after, laid off a town that went by the name of Beason-town, but now Union-town, the capital of Fayette County, Pennsylvania.

1772. Six years of happy days had passed away, my father, having sold his plantation, bought land about fourteen miles from Fort Pitt, on the north fork of Robertson's run. In the year 1774, the Indians broke out. At that time the whites were the aggressors, caused chiefly by the murder of Bald Eagle, a Delaware chief, by some villains on the Ohio, while he was in his canoe, and the murder of the family of Logan, the celebrated Mingo chief, by Captain Michael Cresap. We all had to fortify ourselves. Dunmore, Governor of Virginia, marched an army into the Indian Country, and as the Indians had not done much mischief, soon returned home, after patching up a kind of peace with them, which was however of short duration.

In the interval of peace during the year 1776, my father built a mill on Raccoon creek, on land he had previously purchased ten miles northwest from home, and hired Isaac Felty to keep her that winter. In the spring of 1777, he moved to the mill. In the summer the Indians recommenced hostilities. A few families forted at the mill.

The Indians fired on John Stallions, shooting his mare through, and himself through the arm. She ran with him about one mile to Dallow's Fort and fell dead. This was all the mischief done near us, but the frontiers in other parts suffered more, of which I can not give any account at this time. In the fall my father returned home, and as the Indians lived at some distance, and the winters were cold, we were not troubled with them during that season, so that we all lived at home in safety.

However, in the spring of 1778, all forted again. My father forted at McDonald's fort, two and a half miles from home. During the summer my father obtained a guard of men, to be stationed at his mill, and men would go in companies armed, and get grinding done. When winter set in, the guard left the mill, but the miller stayed till the first of March, and then moved off.

1779. This winter my father was elected Captain and received his commission from the Governor of Virginia, which at that time claimed jurisdiction over all that part of Pennsylvania laying west of Laurel-hill, which claim they held until the year 1782.

Some time in March, the Indians fell on a camp of sugar-makers, and killed five young men, and took five young women and a boy prisoners. This camp was on Raccoon creek, two miles below my father's mill. There was another camp on the creek, one mile below that. My cousin, John Finch, and myself were at the mill during the time the murder was committed, having been sent there by my father on an errand, and being detained there a day or two in consequence of a rise in the waters of the creek. The Indians had discovered the camp, and laying in ambush all night, fell on them about daylight with their tomahawks. This we knew to be the case, as the bodies all lay in and near the camp, except one, who had run about fifty yards, and was there tomahawked and scalped. Two of the young men were of the name of Devers, two named Turner, and one Fulks. One of the Devers lay in the camp, with his shoes on slip-shod. He was stabbed in the left side, and was laying on his right side, with his fingers and thumb, standing [?] on end over the wound. The creek falling, we returned home.

The same morning, a man from the lower camp went to theirs, to borrow a gimblet to tap sugar trees, and found the men killed and the women and boy gone. He gave the alarm to their friends at the settlements ten miles off. The next day we went to bury them. Ephraim Ralph, a cousin of my father's, who was a Lieutenant in the United States service, in Captain Laughery's company, was then at home on a visit, and went with us. When a grave was dug, the men being backward to lay them in it, Ralph told them not to hold back, for they knew not how soon they might be in the same situation themselves. So setting them the example, they were all laid in one grave and buried, and then we returned home.

These were the first I had seen that had been killed by the Indians, and a dreadful sight it was to me, the more so as some of them had been but a short time before my schoolmates. The grief and lamentation of poor old William Turner is still fresh in my remembrance, lamenting the loss of his children, his two sons George and William, that lay there tomahawked and scalped, and his beloved daughter Betsey, a beautiful girl of fourteen years of age, taken captive by the cruel savages, not knowing what she had suffered or might hereafter suffer. His grief can be better conceived by tender parents than described.

In the year 1782 [1781 -- L.C.D.], as Captain Laughery was descending the Ohio in a boat with his company, in order to join General Clark, he landed at the mouth of a creek, below the mouth of the Big Miami; he was there attacked by the Indians and defeated. Laughery and Ralph were both killed. From which circumstance the creek took the name of Laughery, which it still bears.

In the spring of this year, some forted, others lived four or five families together; four families lived with my father. About the first of August, Alexander McCandless, who lived a mile and a half from my father's, in company with a few families, had occasion to go for Mrs. Meek, an old lady about fifty years of age, who lived about six miles off, where a few families were gathered. After staying the time required, he set off home with her. About one mile from her house they were fired on by five or six Indians, from behind a log, situated about twenty yards from the path. The shots missing both them and their horses, McCandless turned round, took the path home, and was soon out of danger. They then sprung towards the old lady, one of them threw his tomahawk and stuck it in a tree near her head, she however stuck to her saddle, and her horse soon carried her safe home.

A few days afterwards, Alexander McNeely and his brother James, both bachelors, who had gathered with others at Robert Shirer's, went home by themselves to work. Their dog beginning to bark in a hazel thicket, they got alarmed, thinking that there were Indians there, and so returned to Shirer's. Alexander got six men to go with him, leaving his brother James there, who was about sixty years of age. The Indians, seeing them go off, followed them, and waylaid the path, behind a large log. When they came opposite them, they fired on them, killing McNeely and four others; one made his escape by running. Shirer was not killed, but in attempting to leap a muddy branch [=creek], he being old and not able to reach the bank, fell in and was taken prisoner.

[About Sept. 1781 -- Bates Collier killed. -- L.C.D.]

Shortly after that, two men that lived at my father's set off in the evening to hunt, taking a path that led to a deserted plantation. They had not proceeded more than half a mile before they were fired on by Indians and both killed. My father hearing the report of the guns, in company with another person, took the path and ran, but soon returned, having found them both killed and scalped. Their names were Bates Collier and Daniel Reardon. Upon these events, all either forted or moved off, my father moving eight miles. When winter set in, all returned home.

After the death of Alexander McNeely, his brother James, being heir to his plantation and other property, went there and lived by himself. One very cold morning, the snow being about half-leg deep, one of the neighbors going to his house to borrow a bag, knocked and called at the door, but receiving no answer, he pushed it open, and going in, discovered the old man lying by the fire dead, with his feet in the fire much burnt. The fire had then burnt down, and how long he had been dead was unknown.

[1782 -- L.C.D.]

And it came to pass in those days, that the devil entered into Colonel Williamson (who lived fifteen or twenty miles west of us) and stirred him up, to raise a company of men, to go against a town of friendly Indians, chiefly of the Delaware tribe, and professing the Moravian religion, who had taken no part with the hostile Indians, and who lived on the waters of the Muskingum. Having accordingly raised his men, he crossed the Ohio and reached the town. As the Indians were friendly, they did not apprehend any danger, so neither took arms nor fled. He told them, that he had come to take them over the Ohio, as he was apprehensive that the hostile Indians would slay them. Being agreed to this, that evening and night the women were briefly employed pounding meal and baking bread, to take [with] them on their journey.

In the morning, having them in his power, in cool blood he ordered them all to go into two houses, the men into one and the women and children into another. He then gave orders to his men, to go and fall on them with their tomahawks. To that some objected, and called on God to witness that they were clear of the blood of those innocent people. However, he found enough willing and ready to accomplish his diabolical design. They went in and fell upon them. When the butchery commenced, two young men that were brothers sat down together, began to sing a hymn, and continued singing till they were murdered. They were all murdered without distinction of age or sex, a piece of barbarity the Indians were never known to be guilty of, disgraceful to any people professing Christianity. The number slain I have no recollection of at this time. He then returned home in triumph. I never heard any person speak of the circumstance, without abhorrence, excepting one poor old dirty Scotchman, named James Greenlee, "Owh mon, its a weel cum don thing, for they suppurted the other Injuns as tha cum and gaad," for which he got no applause from his neighbors.

Although my father's mill was deserted, and the nearest fort was five miles off, yet the Indians never burned it; and as mills were scarce, the people went in companies armed to get grinding done, and my father went and ground for them. Notwithstanding every one either forted or moved off, they all raised corn at home, those that had removed their families returned themselves to the forts, and [they] went in armed companies from field to field, where while some worked, others kept guard.

During the spring of 1780 [1782 -- L.C.D.] my father moved fifteen miles; and it was during the summer that Colonel Crawford's unfortunate expedition took place, where my uncle Joseph Ekeley, who had married my father's sister Susanna and who was a Lieutenant in Captain David Andrew's company, was slain together with his Captain and others of my acquaintance. In the spring of 1781 [1783 -- L.C.D.], my father moved ten miles. There was no mischief done by the Indians this summer in our neighborhood.

Soon after, my father sold his millstones, irons, and bolting cloth, to Josiah Gammel, who at that time was building a mill in the settlement on Chartier creek, and the land on Raccoon, to James Crawford, a Quaker, who was buying land on the frontier for the Quakers. After forting and moving off from home for five years, my father this spring (1782 [?]) moved twenty miles and bought a plantation of William Fry on Peters creek, taking a final leave of his plantation on Robertson's run. All however forted again or moved off, excepting one man by the name of Clock, who lived one mile east of my father's place. One day during the summer, I was sent home on an errand by my father, accompanied by John Woods. We had to pass Clock's house.

When we came there, we saw blood in the yard, but seeing no one, we pushed open the door and went in, and found him and three of his little children lying tomahawked and scalped. One of the poor little things was not quite dead, but lay gaping and sighing. These children were about three, five, and seven years of age. The woman with her sucking child, and the oldest child, a boy about eleven years of age, had been taken prisoners. One little girl, about nine years of age, was at the spring when the attack commenced, and made her escape by running down the spring run, and hiding in the weeds till she thought they were gone, when she ran to Turner's fort about three miles off. The men from that fort pursued the savages, and after following them about four miles, found the little child lying tomahawked and scalped, with its mother's apron spread over it, she not being able to carry it further and keep up with them. Perhaps she might have thought, that by spreading her apron over it, the wolves would not devour it, that they would be pursued, and that probably her child would be found, carried to the fort, and buried. After pursuing them some distance, they found that they could not overtake them, and on their return home they carried the child to the fort and buried it. During this time, there were seventeen killed, one wounded, and nine taken prisoners belonging to our neighborhood.

The five years last past was in the time of the Revolutionary War; the British had taken the Indians for their allies, and paid them for the scalps of men, women, and children, which was the cause of much more murder being committed, than would otherwise have been. The reaction I have here given has been confined to our own neighborhood, but the frontiers west of us, and on the east side of the Monongahela, suffered much of which I can give no account at this time. In the year 1783, my father bought land of John Kiser, which lay in Kentucky. Kiser purposing to go down there in the fall, my father and uncle Finch built a boat, for myself and my two cousins, John and Josiah, to go down with him, take horses and cattle along, and raise a crop of corn for them, as they intended removing themselves the succeeding fall.

I shall now commence a narrative of incidents connected with myself, leaving those connected with my father for the present.

About the twentieth of November, we embarked on the Monongahela in our boat, in company with Kiser, having with us [me -- S.R.] four head of horses and some cattle. We landed at the mouth of Limestone Creek, but there was then no settlement there. We made search for a road, but found none. There was indeed a buffalo road that crossed Limestone creek a few miles above its mouth, and passing May's lick, about twelve miles from Limestone, went on to the Lower Blue Lick, on Licking river, and thence to Bryant's Station, but as we knew nothing of it, we went on and landed at the mouth of Licking river, on the twenty-ninth day of the month.

The next day, we loaded a periogue and a canoe, and set off up Licking, sometimes wading and pulling our periogue and canoe over the ripples. After working hard for four days, and making poor headway, we landed, hid our property (which was whiskey and our farming utensils) in the woods, and returned to the Ohio, which by this time had taken a rapid rise and backed up Licking, so that we took Kiser's boat up as far as we had taken our property and unloaded her. We left on the bank of Licking a new wagon and some kettles. Leaving our property to help Kiser, we packed up, and set off up Licking, and travelled some days; but making poor progress, and snow beginning to fall, with no cane in that part of the country for our horses and cattle, we left Kiser and set off to hunt for cane. He sent his stock with us, in care of Henry Fry, who had come down in his boat with cattle for his father.

When we came to the fork of Licking, we found a wagon road cut out, that led up the South fork. This road had been cut by Colonel Bird, a British officer, who had ascended Licking in keel boats, with six hundred Canadians and Indians. They were several days in cutting out this road, which led to Riddell's fort, which stood on the east side of Licking, three miles below the junction of Hinkston's and Stoner's fork; yet our people knew nothing of it till they were summoned to surrender. [They] refusing to do so, [the British] attacked the fort with cannon, which their stockade not being able to withstand, they were compelled to surrender. A few were killed and all the rest made prisoners. They then proceeded to Martin's fort, six miles higher up Stoner, and succeeded in taking it also.

We took this road, and went on, the snow being about half-leg deep. Early in the morning, about three miles from Riddell's fort, we came to three families encamped. They had landed at Limestone, but finding no road, they wandered through the woods, crossed Licking, and happening to find the road, took it. The night before we came to them, Mrs. Downey was brought to bed. They were poor people, and had not so much as a spare blanket to stretch over her, but were obliged to put up forks and poles, and place brush thereon for a kind of a shelter. She had no necessaries of any kind, not even bread, nothing but venison and turkey. They went to the same station that we did. She had several children, one of them a young woman. She said that she had never done better at any such time in her life. So we see that the Lord is good and merciful, and worthy of praise from all intelligent beings fitting the back to the burden. I have mentioned this circumstance for the encouragement of others; we should in all times of trouble, trial, or difficulty, put our trust in the Lord, who alone is able to save all that put their trust in him.

The names of these families were Reeves, DeWitt, and Downey.

We went on to the fort, where we found plenty of cane. The next morning, John Finch and myself set off to try to find Lexington, and left the horses and cattle in the care of Josiah Finch and Henry Fry, with orders if the snow melted off, or rain fell, to be sure to take the horses and cattle over the river: and as there was no road, we took up Mill Creek, and towards the head of it, we met some hunters, who lived on the south side of Kentucky river, who gave us directions how to find a hunting trace, that led to Bryant's Station. They gave each of us a wheat cake, that had been ground on a hand mill, and sifted, and as I was not well, and had not seen bread for more than two weeks, I thought it was the best bread that I had ever tasted.

We went on, found the trace, and arrived at Bryant's Station. The next day we went to McConnell's Station, about one mile north of Lexington, where there was a mill. We there got the meal we had promised to get for Kiser, and the next morning set off back. It rained almost the whole day. About sunset we came to the river, which was very high. We expected to find the boys on our side of the river, with a good fire; but they had not crossed it, and as they had not obeyed our orders, we knew of no better way to retaliate on them, than to take a journey cake, walk to the bank, and hold it up for them to see it. We did so; they saw it, but did not taste it.

By this time the rain was over, but we were wet and cold; and as it began to get colder, we made a fire, and camped there that night. Early the next morning, we set off down the river, and at night encamped on the bank of Licking. It was very cold, from which we suffered much, and the next evening after dark [we] arrived at Kiser's camp. The next morning, we set off on our return. When we got to Riddell's station, the river had fallen so much, that we could cross it, [and] we therefore went on to McConnell's station, where we arrived the last of December.

Some time in January four of us set out to hunt on Stoner; the buffalo being all gone off, we had to go about twenty miles after them. The second night it began to snow and get very cold. In the morning, the ground was so much covered with snow, that we could not track our horses; we hunted for them, but not being able to find them, we hung up our saddles and started for home, thinking that our horses had gone in that direction. It snowed all day. At night, when we came to Elkhorn creek, the snow was knee deep. We waded the creek, about the same depth, and soon found ourselves in a large cane brake, where we could get no wood to make a fire. The cane was all bending with snow, and no broken wood was to be found. However, we found an old hickory stump, about fifteen feet high. We pushed it down, and it being dry and rotten, we put fire to it. It was all the fire we had that night, but we could not dry ourselves by it.

The next morning we went on four miles to Bryant's station, where when we arrived, our leggings and moccasins were frozen, and some of our feet frost-bitten. Shortly after our arrival at home, our horses were found by hunters and brought in. The snow that then fell was not all off the ground till the tenth of March, and then went off with rain. This was a very cold winter, my horses (with the exception of one) and all my cattle strayed off so that I could not find them.

The tenth of March 1784, John Finch and myself set off after our property we had left on Licking, and found all safe, but had some trouble on account of high water, and were gone ten days.

In the course of this spring, people began to settle in the neighborhood of Lexington. Colonel Garrard settled a station on Stoner, and General Benjamin Harrison settled a station on the same river. I think he was a cousin to the much lamented brave Gen. William Henry Harrison. William McClelling settled a station on the road between Hinkston's and Stoner's forks; and Simon Kenton settled a station one mile north of where the town of Washington now stands, the capital of Mason County, Kentucky. A blockhouse and warehouse was also built at Limestone, which was a great convenience to emigrants as they came rapidly down this spring.

The land my father had bought lay remote from any settlement, and times being dangerous, we could not go on it; we therefore took a lease of Alexander McConnell. We put up a cabin, and four of us lived together, my two cousins, Henry Fry, and myself. We had to get our meat, by hunting deer and turkeys, as the buffaloes were too far off. This spring I was attacked with a fever, and was very bad; after I had got some better, but not yet able to work, I heard of one of my horses at Harrison's station. I went after him, and upon my return home, it rained almost the whole day. I got very wet, and took a relapse, and was worse than I was at first. This put me back so much with my work, that I got but four acres planted, but as range was good and cane plenty, I raised enough to supply my father, till he raised corn for himself.

This spring my uncle Finch came down the Ohio, and lived in the cabin with us. I heard of my mare, about fifteen miles north of Lexington, and found her near a great buffalo road, that comes from the north-west, out of the knobs, and leads to the Blue Licks, crossing North Elkhorn at a place which was then called the Great Crossings, which name it still bears. My two year old colt was found near the Big Bone lick and brought in, so I got all my horses again. In the course of the summer, I made two trips to Limestone, packing rum and iron for Thomas January of Lexington.

I also built a good cabin for my father, and in the fall gathered my corn. A small stockade fort was likewise built at the Blue Licks, to make salt at a spring on the west side of the river, which was most convenient to timber, although the main spring was on the east side.

Sometime this summer, a family landed at Limestone, that had the small-pox, and went on to the Blue Licks. They were not permitted to enter the fort, but encamped on the opposite side of the river. The Indians fell on them in the night, and murdered the whole of them.

About the first of August, I set off to hunt my cattle, accompanied by Alister McConnel. We steered a northeast course till we struck the south fork of Licking. We then steered a norwest [?] course and hunted them three days and then returned back and encamped not far from main Licking, thinking to go to the mouth of Licking. Quite early in the morning, before we came to main Licking, we killed a large buck elk, which we skinned, and hung up the hide. We then took some of the meat, soon came to the river, and went down it. We there saw the fresh track of an Indian, which we followed for several miles.

That evening a heavy shower of rain fell, so that both our guns got wet, which rendered them useless. About sunset we came to Kiser's camp, and encamped there for the night. The Indians had been there, cut his wagon some, and broke some of his kettles. As our guns were wet and out of order, we let them remain so, which I think was providentially ordered; for if we had put them in order that night, which could only be done by picking powder in at the touch-hole and shooting them off, the Indians would have heard them, and have come in search of us, and have found us by our fire.

If we had put them in order in the morning, they would have heard us, as they were encamped not more than half a mile off, which we knew nothing of. When morning came, we thought we would get our horses first, and then put our guns in order. We accordingly left them at the camp, and set out to hunt our horses separately. While we were out, we heard the reports of ten or twelve guns, not more than half a mile off.

When we met, neither of us had found our horses. He said, "Did you hear the guns?" I told him I did. He said, "It is Indians." I replied, that I knew it was. He then said, "They have probably found our camp and are watching it." I told him, that the woods were open, that if they were on this side we could see them, that we had better run to the river bank and look down. Should they be there and not shoot us, we must try to make our escape. We did so, and seeing nothing of them, took up our guns, saddles and blankets, and carried them out of sight of our camp. We soon found our horses, saddled them, and mounted. McConnel asked me if I could find the way home without keeping the river. I answered in the affirmative. He then said, "Go ahead, and make the best of your way, for if the Indians find our trail, they can follow us faster than we can ride; and as our guns are out of order, we cannot defend ourselves, and may be killed." At that time the ground was very wet, with a thick undergrowth of weeds and pea-vines, which made it bad riding, and much in their favor to follow us.

Leaving the river at that place, which we struck no more, we rode four miles to a creek, which we could not ford, being swollen by the rain which fell the evening before; however, by riding up the stream a short distance we came to a place where three forks came together, where we crossed above the forks, and rode up the last fork about one hundred yards in the water. When we came out, we fell on the trail of a large herd of buffaloes that had been feeding; we followed them some distance, to make them [the Indians] think we were hunting, and to try to break them off our trail should they be following us.

About sunset we came to the place where we had killed the elk as we went down. McConnel said that if I would make fire, he would go back on our trail and watch it, to which I agreed. He went back half a mile and returned after dark, and reported that he saw nothing of them following us. We then put out our horses, and as it looked like rain, stretched up the elk hide, and lay down. Soon a heavy shower fell, so that the water ran under us; we were obliged to stand up under the hide till it was over. We kindled up our fire which was nearly out, and gathered up brush and sticks to lay on till morning, which being clear, we concluded to stay there, dry our clothes and blankets, and put our guns in order, as we knew that Indians could not follow our trail, in consequence of the rain which had fallen in the night. Having done so, about ten o'clock we started for home, where we arrived on the evening of the tenth day after leaving it.

The last of the same month, four of us set out to hunt on a small stream, then known by the name of Dry [?] run, about sixteen miles north of Lexington. We there killed the largest buffaloe bull I ever saw slain, which was good beef. This was at the time called bellowing time, when the bulls are following the cows. The calves are all produced at one time in the spring, and when young [they] resemble our common red calves. We skinned the bull, and cut off all the meat in broad thin pieces, which we laid on the hide, and sprinkled salt thereon, letting it lay till we made a long fire. We then put a row of forks on each side of the fire, and placed poles on the forks. Small sticks were then laid on them, and the meat laid on the sticks over the fire, where it remained until half cooked; it was then turned over and left to lay till morning, for by this time it was in the night. We then took our guns, saddles and blankets, slipped off and lay down in the darkest place we could find, for fear the Indians would stumble on us. In the morning we put the meat in bags and carried it home.

Some time towards the last of November, John Finch and myself set out to hunt on Stoner; we met a gang of six buffaloes. He shot one and it fell. The others ran about a hundred yards and stopped. I followed them and shot the leading cow: she fell, the others stood till he came up: we killed the six buffaloes with six shoots [sic], which was the best shooting I ever knew done at buffaloes. It was all good beef. We had each of us two horses, but we could not carry it all, although we carried home the heaviest loads of buffaloe meat, that I ever saw packed. I salted my part for my father.

About Christmas, my father landed at Limestone, and sent me word. I went up to help him move. The first night, we lay at the North fork of Licking, eight miles from Limestone. This stream enters Licking three miles above the junction of the South Fork. The next day I waded Hinkston's fork about waist deep, Stoner's fork about the same depth, and Huston's fork about knee deep seven times. The old buffaloe road went up it, crossing at every bend. At night we encamped in the woods. That evening, I was taken with pains in my back and hips, so that I could hardly walk and carry my gun. That night I lay with my feet to the fire and drank spice-wood tea. The next morning I was broke out thick with the measles. That day I was obliged to ride, and in the evening we arrived at home, where I soon got well.

Before my father left Pennsylvania, he sold his plantation on Peter's' creek to Amos Wilson, on a credit, which caused me to have three trips to Pennsylvania before I got it. He had also exchanged his place on Robertson's run, with Alexander McClelling for five hundred acres of land, six miles west from where Washington now stands, the capital of Mason County, Kentucky.

In February 1785, my father and myself set out to hunt on Stoner. He was a great hunter, and had killed more deer than any man I ever knew; but as he had never killed a buffaloe and as I had killed many, he gave up for me to shoot. We fell in with a small gang of buffaloes, and I killed a good cow, which was good beef, and sufficient for our loads. The way that buffaloe meat was packed, was to split it open lengthwise, and put it on the horse, back foremost; after balancing it, crack the backbone, so that it may hang down on each side, which made a good load to pack. When carried home, it was skinned, the wool sheared off to make clothes, and the hide tanned for shoe leather.

In the fall of this year, William Wood and Arthur Fox laid out Washington; shortly after it was laid out, my father settled there, being the second that settled in it. The reason of his settling there, was in order to get as near to his land as he could.

However, emigrants came rapidly down the Ohio this fall and winter, and the next spring, many of whom settled in Washington. In December I went to hunt buffaloe with two men and took my brother John with me. The first day we found no buffaloe. The second day we went on Fox creek about thirty miles from Washington, and encamped. We set out to hunt in the evening, when I killed a good buffaloe cow, and on my return to camp, I met a gang of buffaloes, and killed the largest and best cow I ever killed. The other men killed nothing. I gave each of them a half a buffaloe. We all had our loads. In the morning, we loaded our horses, and set off home, where we arrived some time after night.

In the year 1786 [See Shane's *Historical Collections*, vol. II, Shanks' *Notes*, pp. 21-22, Marshall's *Kentucky*, 1st ed, 22 -- L.C.D.], the Indians commenced horse-stealing. In March they stole seven horses from Washington. Fifteen of us crossed the Ohio at Limestone, and pursued them about seven miles, when we came to their camp. We saw one of them about fifty yards from the camp, chopping with his tomahawk. It was in the open bottom of a small run, and he had not discovered us. We halted, and divided into three companies; one to slip round to the right hand, one on the left, and the other to stay there, till the two first companies had time to get round. Richard Gaines, one that was left on the trail, fired at the Indian that was chopping, and alarmed them, so that they made their escape. This was attributed to cowardice in him; as it was thought he would rather shoot and alarm them, so that they would run off, rather than risk an engagement with them. However, we recovered the horses they had stolen, and five riding saddles, some other property, and returned home.

About the last of the month, the Indians stole twenty horses from Washington. We pursued them about fifteen miles and encamped. A heavy shower of rain fell in the night, so that we could scarcely follow the trail next morning, the rain having nearly put the tracks of the horses out. We soon came to the knobs of Locust creek. There they had scattered and we could follow them no farther, so that they escaped and we returned home.

This summer we had to get our meat by hunting. Sometimes we had to go twenty or thirty miles after buffaloe, hunt all day and ride after dark, so that if the Indians were dogging us on our trail, they would lose sight both of us and our trail. We would then hobble our horses, take our guns, saddles and blankets, step off some distance from our horses, and lay down in the darkest place we could find, for fear the Indians would stumble on us; sometimes suffering with cold, sometimes with gnats and musquitoes, afraid to make fire; though in the winter we made fire. Deer and turkies were plenty, so that we had sufficient; our bread was made by grinding corn on hand mills. Sometimes we had to stand sentry all night at different parts of the town, for fear the Indians would fall on us in the night. And thus we lived in Washington, two years and four months.

The twenty-ninth day of August, I set off from Limestone for Pennsylvania, after money for my father, in a canoe, in company with Abner Overfield, a man by the name of Blair, and another whose name I have forgotten, four of us, which was dangerous, as we had to keep near shore. We often saw fresh signs of Indians, but did not see any of them. One day a heavy shower of rain fell; we got very wet; after the rain we saw more signs of Indians, and at night it was thought best to lay in the canoe. We had sometimes lain on the bank, and made fire. Getting very chilly, Overfield said, "The Indians are not as thick as trees in the woods; I will have fire." I went with him on the bank, made a fire, and lay by it. The other two chose to lay in the canoe.

Next morning, shortly after we started, we saw the fresh track of an Indian, who had come down the bank to the river. We went on till we came near the mouth of Fishing creek; at that time and place it was about fifty yards from the bank to the water, and we had to keep about forty yards out in the river, it was so shallow. Between us and the beach, we saw a raft laying. I told them to stop the canoe, and I would go and see if it was fresh. Upon examination I came to the conclusion, that they had just crossed on it. Shortly after, we heard as it were, turkies yelping on the banks. Supposing it to be Indians trying to decoy us ashore, as we were too far off for them to shoot us, we went on and passed the mouth of the creek.

Just above the creek was a plantation, and a path down the bank. Supposing that people were living there, I and another ran up the bank, to let them know about the signs we had seen. We found the place deserted.

There was a field of corn with hogs in it, one of which had been just killed by the Indians, whose tracks looked as fresh as our own.

We then crossed the river to the Indian side, and at night we crossed over to a plantation on the Virginia side, where we stayed overnight, and arrived at Wheeling the next evening. The people with whom we stayed the preceding night, were loading a keel-boat to move up to Wheeling, and also arrived there.

In the morning I set off, and went to the man that owed my father the money, but did not get it. I then took water at the mouth of the Youghiogany. This fine little river takes its rise in Virginia, and runs through the north-west corner of Maryland, west of the Allegany mountains, then passes through Laurel-Hill, and part of Fayette, Westmoreland and Alleghany counties, entering the Monongahela in Alleghany county, twelve miles above Pittsburgh [that is, southeast of Pittsburgh, the river flowing northwest -- J.C.L.], by a mouth one hundred and fifty yards wide. I returned home down the Ohio in a family boat.

In May 1787, Colonel Todd came with a company of men from Lexington, to go in search of Indians on the Scioto and Paint creek, and raised some men in Washington.

He crossed the Ohio with his men, one hundred and seventy in all, at Limestone, and proceeded on towards Old Chillicothe, on the North fork of Paint creek. After we had crossed the Sunfish mountain, we fell on a camp of four Indians, three men and a boy. We killed two of them, and took the other two prisoners. That day a heavy shower of rain fell; we all got wet, and at night encamped on an old Indian path. As the moon gave light, thirteen of us turned out, to go in search of an Indian camp, which the prisoner had informed us of. We left our provision and blankets at camp, took the path and went on about five miles, till we came to a small creek. We heard dogs bark, and bells, about a quarter of a mile off, up the creek. We concluded to stay there, slip up to their camp before day, and to fire on them at daylight. We tied our horses, and made a small fire, thinking it best not to make a large one. Two of our men, not thinking it safe to attack them ourselves, set off back for more assistance, and left us sitting round our little fire, hungry, wet and cold. About day-light, about forty men came on; and without making a halt to consult us as to what would be best to do, rode hastily on, so that before we could get our horses and mount, we fell nearly in the rear.

They rode up to the camp, alarmed the dogs; the men all made their escape, so that they only took three squaws prisoners. Flanders Callaway shot an old squaw, which he should not have done. I saw her lying on her face with her back naked. She was much pitted with the small pox, which I think they got among them, when they killed the family at the Blue Licks in 1784. We got horses, and a great many articles, such as twilled bags, pewter &c., which they got by plundering the people as they moved from Virginia to Kentucky.

The rest of the men coming up, the plunder was all divided among the companies. The men raised at Washington composed one company. It [the plunder] was sold at vendue on the spot; our part amounted to forty-three shillings for each man. We then set off for home, and at night encamped on a branch of Sunfish creek, where the Indian man made his escape.

This spring, two men, Smith a Yankee and Thomas a Welshman, set out from Washington early in the morning to hunt their horses, and found them in a cane-brake about half a mile from Washington. The horses were in a small open place, one on each side. Each man went to his horse. Smith discovered Indians about ten steps from him in the edge of the cane, with their guns pointed at him: he had no time to run, but went up to them. They told him to call the other man to come to them. Thomas had not yet seen them when Smith called to him. In place of jumping in the cane and clearing himself, as he easily could have done, he went up to them. They kept them all day in the cane-brake. There were four Indians and a white man, who told them he was taken as a child from Lancaster County, Pennsylvania. After night they went to Lee's Station, about two miles from Washington, and tried to get horses out of a small pasture near the station: but the dogs were so fierce they could not get them. They made several attempts, but they were driven back by the dogs.

They then set off for the Ohio River, and on the river hill, about four miles from Washington, told their prisoners to go home. Thomas set off at the word go, but Smith told them he could not go without his horse; this they refused to give up. He took out his steel tobacco box, and said he would give them that for his horse.

The Indian took it, and was for keeping it and his horse both. Smith told him it was not honest, to keep his horse and box both; he then returned the box to him, saying "Take it." Thomas was calling on Smith to come, but the old Yankee was still contending for his horse. The white man told him he had better go, as the Indians were getting mad, and if he made them mad, they would kill him. [1787 -- L.C.D.] He then set off, and about daylight arrived in town. This was what I never heard of Indians doing, either before or since.

In July I again set off for Pennsylvania after my father's money, and met a company at Stroud's station, fourteen miles east of Lexington. About forty men met, all armed. I met there John Gosset, a young man, with whom I had been acquainted in Pennsylvania. We took a trace, that had been lately marked out, passing the mud lick, at that time a very noted place, crossed Licking, and proceeded on over a very rough and mountainous part of the country, crossing the Great Kanawha at Morris' station, a little below the mouth of Gauley riv[e]r. Above the mouth of this river it is called New River.

We then took an old cut out road, that led to Green-brier Court-house, now Lewisburgh, which was eighty-six miles. At this place the company separated. Gosset and myself travelled in company; we proceeded up the big levels, crossed the Droop mountain, and up the little levels to the Clover lick, keeping Greenbrier river all the way to the right hand. At this lick, we took a trace to the left hand, crossed a mountain, and fell on the head of the Tygart valley fork of the Monongahela river, which we descended. This valley had been settled, but the inhabitants had all moved off, for fear of the Indians, and had not yet returned.

The Monongahela and Tygart both run north, and interlock with the Little Kanawha, Gauley, and Elk rivers in the Greenbrier mountain. Before we came to the mouth of Tygart, we left it on the left hand, and passing through the Monongahela glades, proceeded down to Brownsville. I went to the man that owed my father the money, but did not get it. I took a judgement bond on him, with a stay of execution for one year. I then returned on down the Ohio in a family boat.

This fall [1787 -- L.C.D.], the Indians killed Lot Masters and Hezekiah Wood near Washington [see Shane's *Collections*, III, 152 -- they were killed in spring 1786 -- L.C.D.], when they were hunting, and scalped Thomas Talmage, a boy about twelve years of age at Lee's Station, about two miles from Washington. He was sitting near a fire after night; they had to cook in the daytime. The Indians jumped on him, and took off his scalp, doing him no other injury. He got well, but hair never grew on his head again.

About that same time, hunters set out from Stockton's Station, to hunt on Fox creek. At night they made a fire, and lay by it. The Indians fired on them, and killed one of the Stocktons; the others sprang up and ran. An Indian threw a tomahawk, and hit one of them on the back, but fortunately it was not the edge, and he escaped; but their horses and guns fell into the hands of the Indians. It was supposed that the savages had fell on their trail, dogged them till night and fell on them while they slept.

This winter I learned the art of surveying in Washington with Zachariah Thompson, and bought a compass chain, scale and dividers from David Brod[e]rick, for which I gave him thirty-four dollars, twelve and a half cents. In March 1788, the Indians stole horses from John Kenton's station, two miles from Washington. The horses were in a stable, not far from the station: the door was bolted in the inside with a wooden bolt. Not being able to open it, the[y] uncovered the roof on the side from the station, sufficient for them to get in it, cut the bolt with their tomahawks, and took off the horses. The men heard them at it, but were afraid to go out.

In the morning, one of them ran to Washington. Fifteen of us crossed the river at Limestone, and took down the river till we found their trail; at night we came to White-oak creek, which is a very crooked rapid-running stream. They took an old buffaloe road, which led up the stream, crossing it at every bend, at that time about waist-deep. We had to hold two or three of us together to enable us to cross it. We crossed it eight times that night by moonlight, and twice next morning before sunrise.

The trail then left the creek, and steered a north-east course. We pursued rapidly, and soon came to a place where they had halted and made a small fire, but it did not appear that they had stayed there long: we pursued on, and about noon we came to a place where an Indian had been watching the trail on horseback: we supposed he had discovered us, as he had ridden off at full speed. We ran hastily on about a mile, and came to their camp. The[y] had fled, but their fire was still burning. This camp was large, so they had been there for some time. There were tracks of children in the ashes.

We there held a council whether to pursue them farther or not. Knowing their mode of warfare, and believing that they had discovered us, we were aware that if they thought they could not stand us, they would scatter in the woods and we could not find them, but if they thought they could stand us, they would waylay us in some convenient place, take the first fire, and we might be defeated, as there was but fifteen of us. We therefore concluded to pursue them no further, and so returned home. Their camp was near where Newmarket now stands.

Sometime this spring [1788], I ran a strait line with my compass to my father's land, from Washington, and struck about twenty yards from the spring, where my father afterwards built his house at, which was six miles, and marked the mile trees. This line was some time afterwards cut out, and made part of the road to Cincinnati.

About the same time, John Machir settled a station, half a mile east of my father's land; to this station my father moved, but cleared ground and raised a crop of corn on his own land. We had to get our meat by hunting, and pursue the same course of life, as when we lived in Washington.

In August, I again set off for Pennsylvania after money for my father, and met the company at the Crab Orchard, which place is in Lincoln County, Kentucky. We took the road to the Cumberland gap, being the route by which the Virginians reached the Kentucky and passed over into Powell's Valley. There the company separated; some of us turned to the east, leaving all the waters of Kentucky, Licking and Sandy to the left hand. Jeremiah Meeks, John Woods and myself travelled in company, crossing some of the headwaters of Clinch river, which takes its rise in Tazewell County, Virginia, and runs southwest. It is one of the main branches of the Tennessee, and interlocks with Big Sandy. We then fell on Blue Stone, a small river, which rising in Giles County, Virginia, interlocks with Clinch and Big Sandy, and runs east into New river, above the mouth of Green-brier river. We crossed New River at English's Ferry, and after crossing Green-brier river, proceeded on to Green Brier Court-house.

There Meeks left us, and we took the same route which I had followed the preceding year, and arrived in Pennsylvania, where I collected the money due to my father. I then went to the State of Delaware, to see the place of my nativity, and on my return home, crossed the Susquehanna at Havre-de-grace, where the river is one mile wide. I then passed through Baltimore, and returned home down the Ohio in a family boat, having been four months absent from home.

In the winter, my father built a house on his own land, to which he moved. This was then the frontier house, and continued to be so for two years. About the same time, the Indians stole two good horses from my father, and two from Williams, who lived in Machir's station.

In March 1789, the Indians stole four horses from Machir's Station. Seven of us pursued them to the Ohio River, about eight miles. When they came to the river, they had went in, and gone down in the water, about one hundred yards, where they came out, and then went down about a quarter of a mile, to where they had a raft. The river at that time was out among the trees. When we came to the river, and saw that they had went in, we supposed that they had gone over; and as we had run nearly all the way, we set down to rest.

Shortly afterwards we heard them halloo at the horses, which were not willing to take the river. We jumped up, ran down the river, and soon found their trail. We saw two of the horses feeding, and found a gun and blanket laying. One of our men took up the gun, and said he would take it with him, but he stayed with it, and as we did not look back, we thought they were all coming on. My brother Laban and one more kept along the bank, to see on the river, while I and one more kept about twenty yards out, to see in the bottom.

Happening to look towards the river, I saw my brother with his gun to his face. As we ran to the river, his gun snapped. There were two Indians on the raft, with two of the horses, one tied to the tail of the other. One of the Indians had hold of a halter, while the other was trying to shove off the raft. The horses were about belly deep in the water, and not willing to go farther, which prevented their getting off. Hearing the gun snap, they [the Indians] jumped into the river; one of them made out into the river swimming and diving. Two of the men shot at the other, but missed him, as he was most of the time under water. I fired the instant he raised, and hit him. My brother not being able to get his gun off, as he had come off in a hurry and forgotten his knife, I took his gun out of his hands, and struck the flint with my knife, and when I had her in my hands, gave him the finishing shot.

The other continued swimming and diving, but as the river was out among the trees, we were prevented from seeing whether he reached the other shore or not. If he did, he got no horse, lost his comrade and gun, and got wet to the skin, so that he had not much to brag of.

When the affair was over, three of our men were missing, John Lewis, Joseph Wright, and Dickson Lord. We took the scalp off the one [Indian] that was killed, and with the two horses, returned back to the place where we had found the gun and blanket. There we found the three gentlemen, just come out of their hiding place. Lord tried to apologize, by saying they thought they had better stay there, and if an Indian should escape, he would run to get his gun, and then they would kill him. I told him that they had better went with us, and tried to prevent them [the Indians] from making their escape. One of the horses belonged to Lewis, which we ought to have sold, and divided the money among us four: however, we gave it up to him. The owners of the other horses, not being with us, were glad to get their horses. It was a long time before they [the three] heard the last about hiding in the tree top.

This spring I was elected Captain, and received my commission from the Governor of Virginia, to take rank the twenty-seventh of May 1789.

About the same time, a small station was settled on the Ohio, at the mouth of Lee's creek, about eight miles from us. Sometime in May, Amos Woods and his wife, who lived in the station, came to my father's on a visit, and put his horses in a small pasture near the house. That day I was ploughing near the house, and after dark I put my horses out in the woods, which I did every night, for fear the Indians would steal them. He refused to put his out, thinking there was no danger. In the morning they were gone, and mine safe. The Indians had been watching us, saw me ploughing and thought my horses were in the field. Their tracks were on the ploughed ground, not twenty yards from the house, where they had been in search of them.

Some time after that, Woods crossed the Ohio to hunt: in the evening on his return to his canoe, it was supposed that he discovered Indians, for he was heard to halloo, and was seen running by the people of the station, but they could not help him; he was killed and scalped.

This summer [1789 -- L.C.D.] a gentleman by the name of Coleman came from Virginia to Washington. Having land on Licking, he got Simon Kenton to go and show him his land, and as it was dangerous times, he hired ten armed men to go with him. They set off from Washington, twelve of them, and passing about five miles south of us, fell on to an old buffalo path, that led down Camp Creek. About noon, they came to where the path crossed the creek, slanting down it about fifty yards to the point of a bluff on the left hand side. The bluff was about six feet high, and the ground fell back lower from the bluff. After they had crossed the creek, they turned up it about fifty yards, where the woods were open, clear of under-brush, and plenty of pea vine. There they halted to refresh themselves, and let their horses feed, placing a sentry at the creek. The bluff would completely hide them from the Indians, should they follow them.

That same day I set out to hunt in company with Tobias Woods; when we came to the path, we saw the trail of a number of horses going down it, and not knowing that white men were out, we supposed that Indians had been about Washington, and stolen horses. I said to Tobias, "Let us follow them, and if we can come up with them, we will fire on them, and try to kill a couple of them; probably the rest will run and leave the horses, so we can get them; but if they turn on us, we must run."

Having agreed to this, we threw down our hats, and ran down the path a mile, when we came to the creek. Hearing a horse snort, I said "There they are." We stopped to see that our guns were well primed and in good order. Just as we came to the creek, the sentry saw us. At that time we both had black hair, and [were] bareheaded. Both of us had dark-colored hunting shirts. Supposing us to be Indians, he ran to the company, and told them that the Indians were following them. We caught a glimpse of him running, knew that we were discovered, and treed ourselves to see what we had to do.

The company being alarmed, some started to run: we then heard Kenton halloo, "Stand your ground; not a man run." Knowing it to be the voice of a white man, I halloed and he answered. We went over to them and told them that we had been following them, as we thought they were Indians who had stolen horses. Coleman asked me, what we two thought we could have done with so many of them. If they had been Indians, I told him, we intended to kill a couple of them, and then we thought the rest would run and leave the horses, so we could get them; but if they did not run, but turned on us, then we must run too. He said, if we would go with us, he would give each of us fifty cents a day in cash. I told him we could not do it, for if we did not return home at night, our people would think us killed by the Indians. We went back, got our hats and went on hunting.

Some fifteen or twenty years afterwards, when I was residing in the State of Ohio, which was the last time I saw Kenton, I travelled with him about twenty miles. After talking over many incidents that occurred while we were acquainted in Kentucky, such as hunting, following Indians and the like, he mentioned Woods and our following them that day. He said he thought he had men with him whom he could depend on, from the way he had heard them brag and boast, but he found that if it had not been for him, they would have run and left their horses.

I should have supposed that General Kenton would have known better, from his long acquaintance with men, and living a great part of his life in danger of Indians. It is a well established fact, that the more men brag and boast when there is no danger, the less may be expected of them when they think there is danger.

This brings to my mind a saying of Jane Sproul, a little girl, when we were living in Pennsylvania in 1779. We had left home for fear of the Indians, and were then living at her father's. Her brother Hugh and James Roberts were sitting by the fire, boasting and bragging about what great things they could do among the Indians. After hearing them for some time, she said "It is easy to fight Indians, sitting in the chimney corner, with your bellies' full of mush and milk."

Although this was the saying of a little girl about eleven years of age, it is full of good sense. Had they been far from home, in the Indian country, and half starved, as many a poor fellow has often been, perhaps they might have had different feelings.

About the first of December of this year [1789], Isaac Sellers, my brother Laban's father in law, set out to hunt and took with him a mulatto boy, two horses, and his dog. Overstaying his time, his wife got uneasy, thinking something had happened to him. Shortly after, his dog came home, and then we were satisfied that he had been slain by the Indians.

My brother Laban, John Hughey, and myself set out to hunt for him. The first day we searched on the waters of Locust Creek. The next morning we crossed the dividing ridge, and fell on a small branch of the North Fork of Licking. Going up it, we soon found his camp, where he was lying killed and scalped, his boy and horse taken off. He was lying at the camp on his face, stripped naked. There was a large log within ten feet from the camp; they had slipped up in night behind the log, and when he was kindling his fire in the morning, sprung from the log on him, and struck him in the throat, like sticking a hog.

This we ascertained was the case, as we saw where they had lain behind the log. He had put some small sticks on his fire, which had burned a small hole in the middle and went out. We carried him about a hundred yards, to where a big tree had blown up, and made a deep hole. We laid him in the hole, covered him with a blanket, and cut down all the dirt we could with our tomahawks, on the body. We then placed a large heap of logs over it, to prevent the wolves from getting at it, and then returned home.

1790. I will now relate a dream that I dreamed, though to some it may seem useless, thinking a dream is but a dream. However, I will relate it, and I leave the reader to think what he will of it. About the first of March, I set out to hunt with my brother Laban. We hunted off west about ten miles, and when night fell, went up a small run to its head. After we had encamped, and made a fire, as it was too cold to lay without, we took our horses about two hundred yards off and spencilled them, so that if we should be surprised in the night and not killed, we might get them. We then lay down to sleep, but as it was dangerous times, we kept all our clothes on, except our maccasins, with our shot pouches on, and our guns by our sides, my dog laying by my head.

I fell asleep and dreamed that my brother and I had set out to hunt, and where we had hunted. Our going up the run, encamping, and putting out our horses, laying down with our clothes on, my dog laying down by my head, everything exactly as it had happened. Then I thought that my dog looked down the run and growled, and that the Indians came rushing on to us, and that it was with much difficulty that we made our escape. I awaked, and thought it was but a dream, but soon fell asleep again, and dreamed the same exactly over again, and waked again. My dog then raised his head, looked down the run and growled, just as I had dreamed that he did. I then became alarmed, awaked my brother, and told him that I suspected the Indians were creeping up to us.

I requested him to lay still, till I had raised up and put my moccasins on, and then I would lay down, until he had done the same. I supposed that if we both raised up at the same time, they would think we were alarmed, and rush on us. Having done so, we both jumped up at once, took up our guns, saddles and blankets, and slipped off to the place where we had put our horses, and sat down, it being about day-break, which is the common time for Indians to make an attack. We then got our horses, set off to hunt, and at night returned home. I thought at that time, and think still, that the Indians were creeping up to us.

About the twentieth of March [1790], the Indians were on the Ohio, above the mouth of the Scioto, with two prisoners whom they had taken. John May was descending the Ohio in a boat, with three men, one of the name of Flinn, but the names of the other two I have forgotten, and two young women. As soon as they came opposite the Indians, they compelled the prisoners to go on the bank, and raise a lamentable cry, to induce them to land and take them on board, stating that they had been taken captive, but had made their escape.

But May, thinking it all a deception, made no attempt to land. They still continued to follow him, and he at last being over-persuaded by the women and Flinn, reluctantly consented to land. As soon as the boat struck the bank, the Indians fired on them, killed May and one of the women, and took the rest prisoners.

Before the Indians had left the boat, Thomas Marshall of Virginia, and some other gentlemen, who were descending the Ohio with three boats weakly manned, but heavily laden with horses and store-goods, hove in sight. The Indians sprang on board the boat they had taken, compelling the prisoners to assist them, and being well manned, soon came opposite to them. They then opened heavy fire on them, who finding that they were not able to cope with the savages, either by fighting or running, abandoned two of the boats with their cargoes to the Indians, and all went on board of one boat, and then being well manned shot rapidly ahead. The Indians, seeing themselves fast falling astern, gave up the chase.

Before the Indians could land the two boats they had captured, they fell just below the mouth of the Scioto.

It was soon reported that the Indians had taken two boats, containing 2000 dollars worth of property and 28 horses: whereupon I received orders to raise all the men in my power, and if the men could not be otherwise obtained, to draft one third of my company, and rendezvous at Limestone the same evening with six days provision. This notice was very short, first to try to raise men, then if they could not be raised to draft them, and march ten miles to Limestone the same day.

However, I raised all the men I could without drafting, and marched to Limestone, where we met about one hundred men, the exact number not recollected. We crossed the Ohio the same evening and encamped. The next morning we were paraded by a brave field-officer, whose name I shall spare, and placed in two ranks or lines of Indian file, with orders to march about twenty yards apart, with Captain John Kenton at the head of one file and myself at the head of the other. He himself rode in front on his fine charger, with Doctor Johnston for surgeon in case of need, with my brother Laban in advance as pilot, whom he had selected, knowing him to be a first-rate woodsman. At that time it would seem he had no need of a pilot, as we were to march up the Ohio; however, he found use for a pilot.

We marched on in good order for some time; at length we fell on the fresh signs of a number of Indians; our commander immediately became alarmed, and said to his pilot, "Let us quit the river and take to the hills." He accordingly steered a north-east course, into the hills and knobs, and at length fell on a creek, where more recent traces of Indians were seen. He was again most powerfully alarmed, and said to his pilot, "For God's sake, Records, make to the river." He then steered a south course, to a small creek, and descended it to the Scioto River. At the mouth of the Scioto River we found the two boats that had been abandoned by Marshall and his company. All the property was taken away, with the exception of two new stills, which the Indians had no use for. A great many cakes of chocolate, and papers of pins, lay scattered about on the beach, but spoiled by the rain that had fallen on them.

We went on board of the two boats and arrived safely at Limestone, having been commanded by such a brave, courageous and warlike officer. Of the number of days we were out I have no certain recollection.

> Hard is the heart that cannot feel
> For cowards when distressed;
> Who will not drop one tear of grief
> And pray they may find rest.

On the fifteenth day of April [1790], I was married to Elizabeth Ellred, daughter of John Peter Ellred and Mary his wife. I settled on my own land, six miles west of Washington, where I had previously built a log cabin, sixteen feet square, and cleared some ground. At that time it was the outside cabin west.

I will now give a description of my log cabin, and the way it was built. After raising it the necessary height, a large log was laid across the middle, and overlaid with split logs. Two of the pieces at one corner were cut out, to make a hole to go up above, then built up, so as to have room to load and shoot, with port-holes above and below. The door was made of strong puncheons, pinned with a two-inch pin, and barred with a strong bar, so that it could not possibly be forced open.

Abraham Gardner and Rudolph Fuso took leases of me, and lived in the same cabin with us, as they had no time to build cabins for themselves. They were both Dutch men and not used to guns, so that I could have no dependence on them, only that they would make a show if Indians came in sight; and if we should be fired on, they might be shot at in place of me.

This summer my brother Laban and my brother-in-law John Hughey were employed to spy on the Ohio River. On the second day of August, on a big lick on Locust creek, four miles from the Ohio, they saw the beds of twenty-two Indians, who had been watching the Lick. They sent word as soon as possible to Colonel Rankin, who gave orders to me to draught ten men from my company, and to meet in the morning at my father's, where I would be met by fifteen men from Captain John Kenton's company, and from there to go in search of them.

I raised my men, and met according to orders, but only found six of Kenton's men. However, we set off, nineteen in number, and when we came to the lick, we saw that a number of horses had just gone down the creek. They had been up on Stoner, the south fork of Licking, and had stolen twenty horses.

We pursued them rapidly to the Ohio; they had all got over but four; at that place it was twenty yards from the bank to the water, and growing thick with grass. About fifty yards above, the water came up to the bank, with a thicket of willows growing. An Indian was standing sentinel close to the bank; we saw him the instant he did us. Some jumped down the bank after them; some ran up the bank to keep them down; one made his escape by swimming and diving; two ran into the willows, and we could not find them. My brother Laban killed one that had squatted in the grass. The one in the river had many guns fired at him, but to no purpose, as he was most of the time under water. The other Indians halloed and shot at us, but to no purpose, as the river was too wide. Only one ball reached the shore, by skipping some distance on the water. We took the scalp off the one that was killed, got his gun, and four horses which they had not got over the river, and returned home.

About the first of March 1791, the Indians stole horses near Washington, just before daylight. The horses were soon missed, and they were pursued. Snow beginning to fall, and cover the ground, they were obliged to leave the horses, disperse, and run to make their escape.

John Gardner set out that evening from my house to hunt, and saw the track of one of them, who had come near my fence before he saw it, and then turned short to the left, to go round the field. It was a fine thing for him that I did not know of his coming there. Had I known it, I would have went out, met the gentleman, and given him a salute.

Sometime in March Captain Hubbell was descending the Ohio. Below the mouth of Scioto, he was attacked by a large party of Indians, who came out in their canoes, and fired on the boat, wounding four or five of his men, and killing two, by the names of Kilpatrick and Tucker. They soon gave up pursuing Hubbell, and turned their attention to Greathouse's boat which was then in sight, and as soon as the boat came in reach, attacked it. This boat being weakly manned, surrendered without much assistance. They took this boat to shore, killing Greathouse and a man named Black. How many they took prisoners I have no recollection of at this time.

I went up to help bury the dead, and on our way we met a boy about fifteen years of age, who had been taken prisoner, but had made his escape. He turned back and went with us. When we came to the boat, Black was laying in it, tomahawked and scalped. The boy said, "There lays my poor old father." Greathouse lay on the bank, tomahawked and scalped. There was a large sack of flour, some hogs, and some other property in the boat, which they had not taken off. After burying the dead, we took the boat down to Limestone.

Some time in the year 1792, application was made to my brother Laban and myself, to view a road from opposite Cincinnati to Washington, and cut it out a bridle-path, for a sum of money which the men in Washington had made up, which we agreed to do. Forty miles of it was then an unbroken forest, and as it was dangerous times, we took with us two men armed. We viewed the road down, and cut it back. While two worked, the other two carried the four guns and provisions, keeping at the same time a look out. Having accomplished the job to their satisfaction, we received our pay. It was some time afterwards cut out, and has been for a long time a very public road.

During this summer, the Indians were hunting opposite the mouth of Locust creek, having their camp about four miles from the Ohio River. After killing a number of deer, they needed horses to pack off the skins; and no doubt thinking that should they come into our settlements and steal horses, the horses would be missed and they pursued and overtaken before they could recross the Ohio, as it was only about twenty miles to the mouth of Locust. Now about four miles south of us, the hills set in, forming a very rough and unsettled part of the country, which continued to the mouth of Locust, and so up to the road leading down from Washington to the Blue Licks. Now should the Indians waylay this road and get horses, before the news could be taken to Washington and men collected to go to the place, there would be sufficient time to cross and make their escape, more especially as the men would have no way to cross the river. This was no doubt their scheme.

A certain young man who lived on Stoner was driving a wagon to Limestone, while the Indians were waylaying the road in the knobs of Johnston's creek about fourteen miles from Washington. When he came opposite to them, they sprung into the road before him, took his horses by the bridle, and made him prisoner. They then took him and his horses and set off for the Ohio River, which they crossed after travelling twenty-five miles over a rough hilly part of the country.

As the prisoner had a bottle of whiskey, the Indians drank pretty freely, and got somewhat intoxicated. The roughness of the way, and the darkness of the night, caused them to get bewildered, which retarded their progress, and was ultimately of advantage to their prisoner.

Shortly after he was taken, a traveller came on, going to Washington, and found the wagon in the road and the gears laying. He rode hastily to Washington, and took the news to Colonel Rankin who lived in Washington. He sent off an express to me, ordering me to raise men and pursue them if I possibly could. (Why did he not give orders to Captain John Kenton, who lived only two miles west of Washington, or to Captain Lee, who lived about the same distance east? Perhaps he thought they would be slow in raising men, but knew I would promptly attend to it, and men could be sooner raised on the frontier, than they could about town.)

But the express did not arrive till after night. As soon as it was light, I ran to my brother Laban's and my brother-in-law John Hughey, and sent them after men with orders to meet at my father's as soon as possible, while I ran to others. We soon met ten of us and took the road to Lee's-creek Station on the Ohio, about eight miles off, where I knew an empty flat-bottomed boat lay. We ran hastily down, boarded the boat, shoved off, double manned the oars, and one took the steering oar. We then pulled out into the middle of the river, and pushed on with all our force. We made good headway and kept the middle of the river as long as we could do, for fear of passing the place where they had crossed the river.

We then fell over to the northwest side, then called the Indian side, and kept near the shore to see the place where the horses came out of the river. We soon came to the place, landed, tied our boat, took the trail and pursued them rapidly about four miles, and came to their camp, but they were gone. They had divided about equally into three companies, which made us at a loss which trail to take. We wanted to follow those that had the prisoner, as we were more anxious to release him than to kill them. However, we chose the middle trail, and following it, pursued them hastily about two miles, where they again divided into two equal companies. We were again at a loss which trail to take, but chose the right hand.

The trail by this time was small, but we pursued it as long as we could see and encamped for the night. At daylight we continued the pursuit, and soon heard them halloing, according to their custom upon leaving the camp. We then felt certain of overtaking them, and soon came to their camp, from which they had steered a north course. We followed them about two miles in that direction, when coming to a large tract of fallen timber, that crossed their course, they turned short to the right, in order to go round it, or find a passage through it.

The woods for some distance had been bushy, which prevented us from seeing them sooner, but near the fallen timbers the woods were open. When we came to the turn they had made, we discovered them about sixty yards distant. There were four of them with one horse laden with skins, on which an Indian was riding. Two walked next to him, the prisoner behind, and one brought up the rear. They had taken the prisoner's shirt from him, and given him a calico shirt in its place. He was bare-headed, having his own big coat wrapped up small, hoppised [?] on his back, with his bottle in it: although the Indians had drank his whiskey, he was careful with his bottle.

The instant we saw them, they were alarmed, and started on the run. The one behind the prisoner jumped before him, all running towards the fallen timber, with the prisoner after them. John Hughey fired at the Indian on the horse, who either jumped off or fell off, and made his escape by running in the fallen timber, which was near him, and grew thick with weeds and pea-vine. He left a first-rate new rifle gun laying, by which we knew that he was badly wounded, as an Indian will never leave his gun, so long as he is able to carry it off. We supposed that the prisoner was an Indian, on account of his running off from us, and because he wore a calico shirt. My brother Laban shot at him, but his gun making slow fire, he missed him, but hit his big coat, which had turned under his arm, making sixteen holes in it, and breaking his bottle in many pieces.

At that instant an uncommon incident occurred. Some cried out, "Shoot him!" -- some, "Don't shoot! let us take him prisoner!" On hearing this, he knew that we were white men, and turned, running to meet us, hallooing, "Oh my wagon, my wagon," which he supposed to be the best countersign he could give, as he knew his life was in danger. So he was released from captivity. We asked him why he had run from us; he replied, that he had not thought it possible that white men could be there in such a short space of time, but that he took us for another party of Indians, who were at war with those who had taken him, and thought it best to stay with those who had him already.

We took the horse, pack of skins and gun, and returned to the Ohio, which we crossed in our boat. That night we encamped on the knobs of Locust creek, and the next day arrived at home. As the horse belonged to the prisoner, we gave it up to him, and he went on his way rejoicing. The pack of skins and gun fell to us for our trouble.

If, when that young man had been taken prisoner, the news had not soon been taken to Washington, and then to me; if I had not hastily raised men; if there had not been a boat at Lee's-creek Station; if we had not pursued them rapidly; if we had not taken the right trail each time they separated; [then] the man would not have been released from captivity. And then, if my brother's gun had not made slow fire, if there had not been a division about taking him or killing him; if we had all fired on him; [then] he surely would have been killed. Some may think it all an accident, and indeed it does look like an accident. But, my friends, when we rightly consider, that with the Lord there is nothing accidental, for although the savages were permitted to take him, yet they were not permitted to keep; so it was not possible, that there were any ifs in the case.

The first of June [1792 -- J.C.L.], Kentucky becoming a state, all commissions from the Government of Virginia became null. Some time in November, I was elected Captain again, and received my commission from the Governor of Kentucky; and on the ninth of January 1793, I was sworn into office by John Wilson, a Justice of the Peace.

Some time in the summer of this year, my brother Laban and myself were appointed to view a road from Germantown to Licking River, opposite the mouth of Beaver Creek, to intersect a road from that place to Georgetown. Also to measure it, and mark the mile-trees. We found it nineteen miles and a half, at that time all the way through the woods. We found a good way for a road, which was some time after cut out, and it has been for a long time a public road.

About this time, as near as I can recollect, William McGinnis, who lived half a mile from Washington, was shot down by the Indians, as he was standing in his yard between sunset and dark; but they did not venture to scalp him.

Sometime in the fall of this year, Tobias Woods, Henry Woods, Absalom Craig, and Fielding Fagan, set out to hunt on Locust creek. On their return home, they came to a fine spring that broke out at the foot of a bluff about ten feet high. They encamped there, and set out to take an evening hunt, When they came in at night, one of them said that Laban Records was in the woods, for he had heard him laugh. But as none of them knew of his being out, Tobias was somewhat alarmed, thinking there might be Indians about. About two hours before day, he said, as he had no horse with him, he would set off and hunt home.

At day-light, Fagan went to his horse, and began to unhobble him, and Henry went to the spring. The Indians, who it appeared had fell on their trail, and followed them to their camp, laying in ambush behind a log on the bluff, where they had slipped up to after night, at this conjuncture fired on them, killing Henry at the spring and wounding Craig in the hip. Fagan made his escape and ran home.

I raised five or six men and went with Fagan to the place. Woods lay at the spring, shot and scalped; Craig likewise lay at the camp, tomahawked and scalped. As Fagan said that he saw him running, about fifty yards from the camp, but, being shot in the hip, not being able to escape, we knew that he was overtaken, brought back to the camp, and there slain. We saw where the Indians had lain behind the log, and left a deer skin. We cut a blue-ash sapling and split it. Of this we made shovels, dug up the ground with our tomahawks, and threw out the dirt with our shovels, digging a grave sufficient to keep the wolves from them. In this we laid the bodies, spread a blanket over them, and covered them up. These were the last persons slain by the Indians in our part of the country.

I have mentioned a number of times that the Indians stole horses, and perhaps there were a number that I have no recollection of at this time, as it was so long ago.

In the year 1795 peace was made with the Indians, when I resigned my commission. In August, I set off for Pennsylvania in a canoe, in company with my brother Laban, William Blackmore and David Fink. At the mouth of the Great Kenhawa, we left our canoe and travelled by land. From the mouth of the Great Kenhawa to Belville, the Ohio River is very crooked, making it sixty miles by water. We steered through the woods, being directed by Colonel Lewis, and arrived at Belville at night, and on the next, at the mouth of Little Kenhawa. Next morning we took the road to Clarksburg on the west fork of Monongahela, upon the east bank of the river. This is the seat of justice for Harrison County, Virginia. Forty miles lower down the river stands Morgantown, the county seat on Monongahela County. On the east side, eight miles below Morgantown, Cheat River unites with the Monongahela by a mouth, two hundred yards broad. This river has its source in the Greenbrier mountain, and runs north through a part of Randolph and Pocahontas counties.

Having descended the river to Brownsville, we returned home down the Ohio in a boat. The following August, I set off for Pennsylvania again, in company with Robert Ellrod. We kept up the Ohio by land, and found some difficulty in travelling, having very often to ride up creeks some distance, in order to get above back water. At the mouth of Big Sandy, I was near getting drowned, by attempting to ford it at its mouth. The depth of the water was about three feet, but the depth of the quicksand we could not tell, as we found no bottom. We got about half way over it, but there was no chance of crossing it, as it still got worse. With much difficulty, we got out at the side we went in at, and proceeded up the river about two miles, where we found a good ford with a rocky bottom, and crossed over in safety.

We arrived in Pennsylvania about the last of the month. Some time in October, Zanes who had been employed by the United States to view and cut out a bridle path from Wheeling to Chillicothe, being at work thereon, we, in company with two other men, took that road, and came up with them about ten miles from Chillicothe. We then steered through the woods to that place, and then reached home, after an absence of sixty days. We were the first persons that ever travelled that road.

1800, June 23rd. I sold my plantation in Kentucky, and in August myself and wife set off for Pennsylvania. We followed Zanes' road and arrived there about the first of September. Shortly after our arrival, we both took the fever and ague, and both had hard shakes every day. Not being able to ride home, we took a passage in a boat laden with apples and cider, bound to Limestone. The river was so low that we were sixty days on it, and each of us had a hard shake every day. When we landed, we were hardly able to ride home, and had the ague almost the whole winter. I had more than one hundred hard shakes, without missing one day, and many afterwards.

In March 1801, I moved to the State of Ohio, and settled in Ross County, on Sunfish creek, where I had previously bought land. I there built a grist- and saw-mills.

1803. I was appointed with two other men to view a road from Newmarket to the Scioto salt works. Forty miles of it, was at that time through the woods. The other men not being woodsmen, it fell on me to lead. We found a good way for a road, which was some time after cut out, and became a public road.

1804. I was solicited to be candidate for Captain, to which I objected; however, as I did not attend the election, I was run in, and received my commission from the Governor of Ohio, which I returned to General Mossie, letting him know, that it did not suit me to serve.

1805. I bought land on the wet fork of Brush creek, in Adams County, now Brown, and in April moved and settled on it, and there built a grist mill.

In the year 1821, I sold my plantation in Ohio, and moved to the State of Indiana, where I settled in Bartholomew County, six miles north of Columbus. Here we suffered a great deal from sickness, and lost four of our children.

1833 was the last year, I was able to farm my plantation. I then rented it for three years. The rent was sufficient to support us, but we were neither of us able to do the work which was required to be done; and as our children were all married, and left us, they advised us to break up house-keeping and live with some of them. This I was reluctant to do, but as there seemed to be no alternative, about the last of November 1836, we went to live with our son-in-law Tunis Quick, and our daughter Susannah, with whom we still [1842] reside.

We have had thirteen living children, and one still-born. We have had eighty-seven grand-children, but twenty-one have departed this life. We have had seven great-grand-children, two of whom have departed this life.

[APPENDIX]

I will now give the names of our children, the dates of their births, marriages and deaths.

Isaiah was born on the tenth day of April 1791, and married Mary Alexander on the eighth day of April 1813.

John was born on the sixth day of July 1793, and married Rachel Bayley on the twenty-eighth day of March 1817.

James was born on the 25th day of July 1795, and married Elizabeth Heaton on the 23rd day of October 1820, and departed his life on the 23rd day of September 1823.

Hannah was born on the fourteenth day of July 1797, and married John Wilson on the twenty-ninth day of December 1814.

Laban was born on the sixth day of September 1799, and married Hannah Bradley his first wife on the nineteenth day of September 1822, and married his second wife Elizabeth Ann Barnet on the twenty-fourth day of February 1825.

William was born on the twenty-third day of November 1801, and married Elsie Harvey on the 17th day of March [no year -- J.C.L.].

Mary was born on the twentieth day of December 1803, and married James Brick on the second day of July 1822, and departed this life on the 17th day of October 1823.

Susannah was born on the twenty-third day of November 1805, and married Tunis Quick on the third day of September 1823.

Matilda was born on the 12th day of October 1808, and married Josiah Hendrickson on the 13th day of August 1833.

Rachel was born on the 27th day of December 1810, and married Milton I. Nelson on the 16th day of December 1830.

Elizabeth was born on the twenty-fourth day of May 1813, and departed this life on the 18th day of October 1823.

Lucinda was born on the 4th day of June 1818 and departed this life on the 10th day of August 1827.

My father departed this life in June 1809, and was buried in his own orchard, aged sixty-seven years. My mother departed this life at her daughter Elizabeth Hughey's in May 1824 and was buried by the side of my father, aged eighty-one years. My father and mother had twelve living children, and one still-born, of which I was the first-born. Their names were Spencer, Nicy, Laban, Joseph, John, Elizabeth, Josiah, Sarah, Mary, Susannah, and William, who have all departed this life except myself, John, and William.

APPENDIX NO. 1

In 1778, General McIntosh marched an army into the Indian country and built a fort just below the mouth of Big Beaver Creek, thirty miles below Pittsburgh, which he called Fort McIntosh. This fort was located on the same ground where the town of Beaver now stands. The same winter, my father received public money to purchase grain, to take into his mill for the use of the army. A great many beef cattle were taken over the Ohio and left on Raccoon creek, to shift for themselves, but as the snow lay on the ground all winter, they all died. I saw some of their hides taken to my father's mill. In the spring he disbanded the army, and went no further. There was also a block-house about half-way between Fort Pitt and Fort McIntosh, where men were stationed in time of the war.

APPENDIX NO. 2

As I have mentioned forts and forting, I will for the information of those that never saw a stockade fort, describe one, and lay down a plat thereof. In the first place, the ground is cleared off, the size they intend to build the fort, which was an oblong square. Then a ditch was dug, three feet deep, the dirt being thrown out on the inside of the fort. Logs, twelve or fifteen inches in diameter and fifteen feet long, were cut and split open. The top ends were sharpened, the butts set in the ditch with the flat sides all in, and the cracks broke with the flat sides of other[s]. The dirt was then thrown into the ditch and well rammed down. Port-holes were made high enough that if a ball should be shot in, it would pass overhead. The cabins were built far enough from the stockades to have plenty of room to load and shoot. Two bastions were constructed at opposite corners (2 x 3) with port-holes about eighteen inches from the ground. The use of these bastions was to rake the two sides of the fort, should the Indians get close up to the stockades, so that they could not shoot them from the port-holes in the sides. Two gateways were made fronting each other (4 x 5) with strong gates and bars so that they could not be forced open.

Some forts had a bastion at each corner. Some forts, sometimes called stations, were built with cabins all set close together, half-faced, or the roof all sloping one way with high side out, raised eight feet high, and overlaid with split logs. The upper story was over-jutted two feet, and raised high enough to have plenty of room to load and shoot, with port-holes both above and below. The use of the over-jut was to prevent the Indians from climbing up, should they get close to the wall, and from it they could shoot down on them. Such was Bryant's Station.

APPENDIX NO. 3

Some time after Braddock's defeat, while the Indians were murdering and committing their cruel depradations on the frontier settlements of Virginia, two girls, sisters of the name of Barnett, the younger six years old and the elder some years older, were taken prisoners by the Indians. The oldest soon became reconciled to stay with them, and some time after married one of them. The younger, although but six years of age, never could be reconciled to stay with them; she never forgot the white people, her own name, and the name of the place she was taken from, but thought that if ever an opportunity offered she would try to make her escape and get home. After having been a prisoner twelve years, she being then eighteen years of age, and there being peace at that time with the white people, she thought she would try and make her escape to Fort Pitt, now Pittsburgh, where the Indians often traded. But no good opportunity offered, as they never took her near there.

However, one morning it was impressed on her to leave them, and an opportunity occurring so that she could slip off undiscovered, she hoppised her blanket on her back and took the course she saw the Indians take when they went to Fort Pitt. She travelled all day, and when night came, she looked round for a sapling that had forks and limbs, so that she could sit thereon, being afraid of the wolves. She thought she could tie herself with her hoppis string, so that if she fell asleep she would not fall. She was not able to find one that answered her purpose, till it began to get dark; she then saw at a distance before her the light of a fire. Going up to it, she found an old Indian man and his squaw, who were on their way to Fort Pitt. The old man received her kindly, supplied her with provision, and conducted her safely to Fort Pitt.

She was then among her own people, who gave her clothes, and dressed her like other white women, and assisted her so that she arrived safely at home. Shortly after her arrival, she gave a Christian experience to a Regular Baptist Church, was received and baptized. Some time afterwards she married Thomas Cummins, and lived a near neighbor to my father, about fourteen miles from Fort Pitt.

In 1774, Dunmore, Governor of Virginia, marched an army into the Indian country and held a treaty with them. They promised to bring in all the prisoners they had into Fort Pitt, which they did next spring. They brought in Susannah Cummins's sister. Cummins went to Fort Pitt and took her home, where she stayed a few days, but not being reconciled to stay, Cummins took her back to Fort Pitt, and she went off with the Indians.

I have made a remark on this circumstance, which will probably not be concurred in by many. However, let that be as it may; I have ventured to make it. Although the Lord did permit the Indians to take her [Susannah], it was not his will that she be reconciled to stay with them. But when his own appointed time came, he impressed on her mind to start the day she did. If she had started the day before, or the day after, she would not have met with the old man at night; she might have missed her way, wandered through the woods, and perished. But that could not possibly be the case. The Lord not only impressed on her to start, but caused the Indians to give her an opportunity to make her escape, and directed her way so that she should meet with the old man at night, caused him to receive her kindly, and conducted her safely to Fort Pitt.

Perhaps some may say what an accident it was that she ever got home. If any of you think so, you are very much mistaken; there was no accident in it. Some may ask this question and say, Why did the Lord have more compassion on her than on her sister? Should any of you ask that question, I will ask you, Why did the Lord choose the Children of Israel from among all the nations of the earth, and give them his laws, commandments and statutes, leaving all the other nations in heathenish idolatry? I could answer your question, I think correctly, but if I did, you might say, I was too much of a predestinarian for you. Yes, and so are the apostles and prophets.

As to my political principles, I am a true Whig. The sin of loco-focoism, I have never been guilty of. In my religious principles, I am a Regular Baptist, having believed in that doctrine for more than fifty years. At this time, myself and wife both belong to the Lewis-creek church of Regular Baptists.

Notwithstanding that I believe that the Evangelical doctrine is neither preached nor believed by any denomination on earth, except the Regular Baptist, yet I would not have you to understand, that I think none will be saved but the Regular Baptists. No, I believe the Lord has a people among other denominations that he will save, but not according to their Arminian principles, which are Antichristian, and always stand opposed to free grace. But all that have been quickened by the Spirit and brought from death unto life, will be saved of every sect, or if belonging to none.

[ADDITIONS]

Josiah departed this life on Monday the 22nd day of May 1848 aged 46 years, one month and twelve days. His wife Mary departed this life on Monday the 22nd day of August two [three? -- J.C.L.] months after him.

1849. My wife and myself have lived together a-going on sixty years since the 15th of last April. I am in my eighty-seventh year since the eleventh day of December last.

# THE REMINISCENCES OF STEPHEN BURKAM

From Stephen Burkam, Ohio County, Virginia, born in January 1762, in Berkeley County, Virginia:

In the fall of 1768, Solomon Burkam and family settled near Beeson's Fort (Captain Jacob Beeson). About 1770 the Indians were threatening, and the scattering people moved over the mountains, except Beeson and those with him. A treaty was soon made without much damage being done, and the people in a few weeks returned. [He] recollects about Colonel Crawford going to the relief of Hanna's Town.

Beeson settled his fort in 1768.

In 1774, Captain William Linn raised a company around Beeson's and Redstone, and went out either with McDonald or Dunmore. In 1777, Linn was sent with Foreman to Wheeling, just after the attack on Wheeling -- had a company -- Linn tried to dissuade Foreman from going under the hill, and he kept above.

Simon Girty early in the Revolution ran against Crawford for some military command, and getting defeated, and a Tory, joined the Indians. Simon was not in the attack on Wheeling in 1782. George Girty was there, and said Simon was then at Kentucky, and George commanded the Indians. Captain Pratt commanded eighty British, and Girty said he had two hundred Indians. Girty made a talk, said he would have the fort, and desired a surrender. He made the speech from the hillside, as soon as the enemy appeared. Pratt spoke after dark.

My informant was out with McIntosh -- 1500 Militia and 500 Regulars. [They] went out in the fall, [and] got back about New Year's -- four months service. General McIntosh was second in command. [They] rendezvoused at Pittsburgh. Colonel Gibson was along. Colonel Campbell from Virginia commanded a Virginia regiment, and was since the War overseer of the penitentiary.

[They] built Fort McIntosh, and then marched about ninety miles to the Tuscarawas, and there erected Fort Laurens. [They] never saw an Indian all the time. McIntosh took Captain White Eyes and Bob Bee, as pilots. Captain White Eyes at Fort McIntosh was taken with the small-pox, and was sent to Pittsburgh, where he soon died. Bob Bee deserted at Fort McIntosh. None other had small-pox.

After reaching Fort Laurens, provisions began to fail, and [they were] put on short allowance -- [a] quarter of a pound of flour each per day, nearly two weeks thus allowed, and finally the main army (seventy or eighty left in the fort) marched on [their] return, without a particle of anything, but the hides left (of the beeves for the army) to dry going out, [they] roasted and ate them.

The ensuing winter, a party of eighteen men went from the fort to hunt the pack-horses, to go to the settlement, for provisions. All were cut off. The ensuing spring, the Militia [were] raised, and went out and escorted in the garrison at Fort Laurens. [They] met with no opposition. Reason Virgin was one of the captains of the escort, and David Shepherd may have been along.

## WILLIAMSON'S MORAVIAN CAMPAIGN

[They] rendezvoused at the mouth of Indian Wheeling. James Marshel was Colonel Commandant of Westmoreland, and Williamson was Second Colonel, and he took command [of] about four hundred men. [They] forded the river (Muskingum). [He has] no recollection of anyone swimming over for sugar, though. [He has] no recollection about the vote [on killing the Moravian Indians -- J.C.L.]. Williamson said, "Do as you please with the prisoners," and picked up his gun and tomahawk and went off into the bushes. William Welch, an Irishman, tomahawked seven. The house was crowded with men tomahawking. The Indians had previously sang and prayed.

John McCulloch was out [as] a private, and seeing two Indian lads, down by the river, when the men were approaching the town, [he] told them to go and hide themselves. They ran off and may have been subsequently killed in the Council-house. [We] reached the town in the afternoon and the Indians were tomahawked a little after dark. Hugh Cameron's hat and hunting shirt were found in one of the houses. These were identified. My informant well knew them. [He] don't recollect about Wallace, nor the cleaned [?] Indian. Next day [they] started back. This was about the latter end of March.

## CRAWFORD'S CAMPAIGN

In May, 489 men rendezvoused at the old Mingo Town. [They were] there a few days. Crawford was chosen by a good smart majority. A good many wanted Williamson, but Williamson himself said he preferred Crawford should be chosen, as he was the oldest man. Still, some voted for Williamson. [There was] only one election. Williamson was second in command, probably McClellan next; Captain Ezekiel Rose (on Ten Mile Creek); Captain Brenton; Major Harrison; Captain Eleazar Williamson; Captain James Dunn [?] from Shirtee; Captain Joseph Bean; Captain John Biggs.

On the way out, three Indians were seen, perhaps by the pilots. [They] escaped.

While marching, [they] saw a large party of Indians making for a skirt of woods, and the men reached there first -- then [they] commenced the fight, and fought till dark. The Indians occupied the high grass, much of it as high as their heads. [They would] only show themselves to fire, and then squat and load. Major Harrison was killed that afternoon, and Captain Munn [?] wounded. Five or six only were killed. Munn had his leg broke but [was] brought in on the retreat, and Captain Bane was wounded the first day. The horses were tied to bushes and trees in the skirt of woods. Provisions etc. were thrown together. Firing ceased about dark. [They] camped, put out [a] strong sentry, and were not disturbed in the night.

Firing commenced early in the morning. [They] kept the same position all day. The fighting was by "little flirts" -- but few of Crawford's men [were] killed or wounded. That afternoon Colonel Williamson requested two hundred men to rush out and attack the enemy. This was denied. [Crawford] thought it improper to divide the men. Just at dusk the enemy was strongly reinforced (Ben Newland with them, who shortly after joined the whites, and made the "leap").

Now Crawford ordered the men to retreat -- each to shift for himself. Colonel D. Williamson tried to keep the men in a body and fight as they retreated. They mostly kept in a body -- commenced retreating just after dark. [They] were followed immediately by the Indians, [but they] were not fired on the first night. In passing the swamp, some stuck fast and had to abandon their horses. Others were overtaken and tomahawked.

The next day (the 6th) there were several little fights. In one [of them, one] of the men, John Hays, was wounded. The next day the Indians caught him, and "ringed" around for his scalp, when they were beaten back, and [then] the third day of the retreat, he was killed. The second day of the retreat (7th June), [there] were three little skirmishes, and the next day, as many more. The last day, Thomas Ogle had his back broke by a ball. He said, "Tell Brother Joe" [Captain Joseph Ogle] "that you left me here, lord of the soil -- I'll keep my tomahawk, [I'll] feign dead, and when they come to take my scalp, I'll fix one of them." He was left to his fate.

The retreat was slow, some days not accomplishing over ten or twelve miles.

The most of those who separated from the main body for safety got killed -- Captain John Biggs and Lieutenant Ashby [among them]. [They] disbanded at the old Mingo Town. Rose, Bane, and Munn [were] all wounded, and all got in. My informant was out both with Williamson in March and with Crawford.

## FIRST SIEGE OF WHEELING

It was John McCulloch who rode down [on] the three-year-old gray mare; [he] often told my informant so, and pointed out the place. McCulloch kept the old mare till thirty-three years old, and [she] finally dropped dead under the saddle, fat as a bear.

There was a large party from Short Creek -- Captain Francis McGuire, Major Samuel McCulloch, and John Green were chased on to Capteen Island [Captine -- J.C.L.], and escaped and reached Van Meter's Fort.

Elizabeth Zane did carry powder at the first siege. [He] heard many who were there say so. She was not at the second siege. [He has] no recollection of hearing about Colonel Andrew Swearingen going there with some men.

## LEWIS WETZEL

Wetzel, about 1785, went out alone in hunt for an Indian camp. [He] went to Stillwater, and there found a camp of three Indians. [He] hid in the bushes, and when they were asleep he crept up and tomahawked all three. [He] took their scalps and guns and went to Wheeling. So he himself told my informant.

When out after Mills's horse, [Wetzel] killed three Indians. [The] Indians called upon him to surrender and yet were themselves tomahawking

Mills, who was shot in the thigh and [it was] broke. The Indians' bodies [were] not found.

When Lewis and Jacob were taken, it was frosty weather, white frost [illegible], and Lewis went back and got his father's gun, then went and got some moccasins, while Jacob was hid in the woods.

The old man, John Wetzel, was alone when killed.

Lewis nor any of his brothers were out with Crawford.

BEN ULIN

Ben Ulin was out hunting for his horse, at or near the mouth of Kenhawa. [He] was pursued by Indians and cornered, and had to jump over a ledge of a great distance into the Ohio River below, and always thought he would have been killed but that he caught hold of a limb of a buckeye sapling, which broke off, but broke his fall, and saved him. He told this to my informant.

In peace, he saw some of the Indians who witnessed the leap. They laughed at him, and asked him why he had not rather be taken than to have ventured such a jump. He said he had rather be killed than taken. This was after 1782. [He] came to the whites, married a wife, and settled down the Ohio.

SECOND SIEGE OF WHEELING

On Sunday preceeding the attack, Ebenezer and Jonathan Zane and Stephen Burkam returned from Stillwater, where they had been to get Indian horses, but [they] got none, and were chased all the way to Wheeling. As to Mills being wounded, [that] is correct -- seventeen wounds and two skips. Henry Smith [was] slightly wounded in the thigh. It was two months before Mills was able to get about. Dr. Knight came once from Pittsburgh to see him. He (Mills) desired Burkam to tomahawk him, to deprive the Indians of that fun, in case they should get the fort. [The] Neisinger and Lefler affair [was] as Mrs. Cruger says.

The siege commenced on Wednesday afternoon, either the 15th or 16th of September 1782.

Peter Neisinger and Hamilton Carr went out spying, as Mrs. Cruger says. Neisinger brought in the hind quarters [?] and came in. [The] Indians crossed at Boggs's Island -- the main body. Some got on to Wheeling Island. A few days before, Andrew Zane had brought two ten gallon kegs of whiskey from Cat Fish Camp, and when within two or three miles of Wheeling, he saw signs and took off and hid his kegs in a tree top.

On the day of the attack, Andrew Zane, Stephen Burkam, Solomon [?] Wright, and half a dozen others went for it. [They] saw the old sign, but nothing more, and got to the fort spring, and were drinking, when the two spies came in. All went to work preparing for the siege. All hands carried water from the river. Sun near two hours high, [they] came beating the drums and paraded themselves along the hill. Then [they] ceased [the] music, and Girty with flag in hand made his speech. [He] promised good usage, stated his strength (that Simon had defeated the Kentuckians at the Blue Licks -- this he said the second day, and said a runner had just arrived with the intelligence), and next day a reinforcement with artillery would arrive.

Burkam fired three shots at Girty, but did not hit him. The swivel was shot -- grape shot and bullets -- and ten Indians scattered, mostly into the cornfield among the corn. [There was] moonlight perhaps a while, but [mostly] a heavy fog. Pratt speaks, said he was a Scotchman, closed by wishing no harm. Betsey Wheat and George Girty confabbed. Girty asked if they had whiskey. Yes, plenty of it. How was it made? In a melting ladle, and you shall have a belly full of it. Said Girty, "I'll have the fort before morning, or go to hell." "Hell, then," said Betsey, "is your portion, for into the fort you cannot come." Then commenced a mutual throwing of stones. After a little, [they] commenced firing on the fort.

Archibald and George Carr, brothers of Hamilton, and Anthony Rigger, and George Scott were also among the defenders. Silas Zane and Andrew Scott were at the fort, and only Ebenezer Zane, Green, and the negro at Zane's house.

Daniel Sullivan and two men, with a load of cannon balls and despatches from Pittsburgh to General Clark reached [Wheeling] just before the siege commenced. Sullivan knew Girty personally and recognized his voice. Sullivan was wounded the first night. [The bullet came] in at the toe, and lodged in the instep, and had it extracted at Pittsburgh, where he went after losing his load. But Sullivan fought.

Two pickets fell, were put up, and a board nailed across on the inside. John Tate and Conrad Stoup [were] gunners. Tate had been in the army. (Captain Boggs sent for aid to Colonel James Marshel, on Buffaloe, etc.)

[They] fired the cannon at Jacob Rigger's house, in which Indians were [hiding], cut the joints in two, and the whole loft fell. [The] Indians scattered out. [The enemy] tried to fire the fort with flax, but failed.

At Zane's house, "Old Sam," the negro, was slightly grazed. He pulled out his plug and fired out, saying "Take care! Sambo is here!" They kept away from Zane's house the remainder of that night.

Next day, [they shot at a] Negro [with the Indians -- J.C.L.], wounded him, and he surrendered and came in. [He] had been taken on Clinch, had on Major Harrison's coat, with a bullet hole through it.

[The] Indians put on petticoats. [They] killed sheep, cattle, [and] hogs, [and] took horses. Not much [was] done that day. [They] would kill cattle, and cut out and cook the tongues. [There were] eleven horses and twelve cows in the fort. One of the latter was shot, etc. That evening, the enemy fired their wooden cannon, within fifteen steps [= yards -- J.C.L.] of the fort, and [it] busted. At Muskingum, on their way out (the negro said), they made one, and wrapped it with elk tugs, and made some noise, but this with chains that did not give. [The] second night, [there was] some firing.

Fiday, about noon, [they] last were seen on [Wheeling] island. [The] men then ran out of the fort and fired on them. Tate (an Irishman) seized the wooden cannon and shouldered it, hollowaing out, "Tell your master that you left an Irishman running off with your cannon."

Colonel Williamson did not come till late in [the] day, marching with some forty men.

On Saturday, Rice's Blockhouse [was besieged] by a part of this enemy. Sunday morning early, forty men (among them my informant and Moses Shepherd), under Captain Ezekiel De Witt, went from Lamb's Fort, some two miles off, and went and followed the trail some distance. [He] don't think Rice went from Lamb's during Sunday night.

# APPENDIX I:
# PETER HENRY'S
# OTHER NARRATIVE

The Peter Henry Narrative exists in two forms. One is the Samuel J. Rea interview (1855) in Draper MS 12E 254-57. Draper purchased the Rea Papers in 1856. The other is the Robert Orr interview (1851), taken at Lyman Draper's own request. This includes answers to a set of queries prepared by Draper. Peter Henry (1769-1858) and his sister Margaret Henry (1771-1853) were taken captive in 1779. The Rea account is printed, with the editor's annotations, in Louise Phelps Kellogg, ed., *Frontier Advance on the Upper Ohio* (Madison 1916). The Orr account had not been published until its appearance in this volume.

It is indicative that Margaret Henry never learned to speak English, though twice married (a Mr. Stoner and a Mr. Haines) and resident in western Pennsylvania. Her recollections, obtained by Mr. S. C. Carpenter for Draper in 1850, are in Draper 8NN67. In one passage she recalled that her brother in fact tomahawked the dead Indian (8NN67): "One of Brady's men gave Peter a hatchet or tomahawk, and he knocked all the teeth out of the dead Savage, and nearly cut off his head." Louise Phelps Kellogg, in her edition of the Rea account (p. 378), suggests that Peter may have later been ashamed of this act. The Rea accounts follows.

\* \* \*

I was twelve [ten -- J.C.L. from L.P.K.] years old at the time of our capture -- my sister was taken with [me]. We were taken about three miles from Pittsburgh on the road towards the latter town [from Greensburg -- J.C.L.]. The Indians killed my mother and all the children except myself and sister. It was early in the day, just after breakfast, when the savages came. My father had gone to mill early in the morning. When he came back, he found everything destroyed.

I am now about 85. My sister was younger than me. I was the eldest of all the children, she next. I did not see the other members of the family killed. They caught me near the door and kept me outside whilst they killed and murdered.

When we were retaken, we were put into a canoe and taken from the mouth of the Mahoning to [Fort] Armstrong, and from thence to Pittsburgh. The Indians had taken five horses and a great deal of plunder, and were several days on their way to Mahoning. There they thought they were safe, judging from the noise they made.

My sister rode on one of the horses. I walked. They did not abuse us; they were kind to us. They had killed a bear and two deer, and had kindled a large fire to jerk the meat at. It was becoming fly blown.

There were nine of them when we were taken; but after they crossed the Kiskiminetas, two of them left. I believe them to have been whites. When Brady attacked them, there were seven of them.

The attack was made just at daylight. We lay quite a distance from the fire when the attack began. I did not know that it was to be made before it was made. I did not see Brady or any of his men the night before. The whites came round the fire in a kind of circle and fired on the Indians at random. There was only one killed on the spot. A number of them were wounded, as could be seen from the blood on the grass, but the whites did not follow them any distance. I was awake when the attack was made. I did not think Indians would fire upon Indians, and was not therefore afraid. My sister did not halloo to the white men not to shoot us.

As soon as the Indians ran off, a German by the name of Joseph Buck came to us and spoke to us in German. I had no English then. I understood from Buck that there [were] twenty-four men with Brady at that time. There was an Indian with Brady's party. The whites gathered up the Indian meat and breakfasted on it. They wanted me to scalp the dead Indian, but I would not. My sister did not go near the dead Indian.

The Indians had taken their horses up into a little bottom the evening before, and tied them there. The whites found out from [me] where they were. They went first and got four horses, but at last they found the mare and her colt. The Savages lost everything. They had stacked their arms at the side of the fire where the whites made the heaviest attack. The whites came down the hill side. Their camp was not just at the junction of the Allegheny and Mahoning, but close by. The fire was about a rod from the creek.

The Indians had killed none but our family at the time they took us. Whilst they were going in, they killed a militia Captain. Brady knew this party had done it from the fact that his coat was found among the spoils taken from them. A company came from Westmoreland for the purpose of getting myself and sister, and they took us from Pittsburgh to Westmoreland. Parkman and Nicholson were two of Brady's men. [James] Amberson, who formerly lived on the old Franklin Road on Canaquanessing Creek in this County [Butler], was also there. My sister is dead; she died about two years since.

# APPENDIX II: RECOLLECTIONS OF RACHAEL JOHNSON

Old Rachael was in both the sieges of Wheeling. Mrs. Cruger, near Wheeling, became acquainted with Rachael Johnson in 1781, then comparatively an old woman -- had four children and was always truthful, and worthy of full credit. She died in the summer of 1847. -- L.C.D.

## BEFORE THE REVOLUTION

[She] says she recollects well the talk consequent upon Braddock's defeat -- and seeing the recruiting officers go around to raise men for Forbes's campaign -- beating the drum, and exhibiting the bounty money. When Washington visited his lands, etc., on the Ohio, below Wheeling, at the mouth of Fish Creek, she saw him at her old master's, Mr. Yates Conwell's, where Washington dined, and Rachael says she ate off the same plate immediately after Washington. This was about 1773 -- or not long before the Indian War of 1774.

[She] thinks she forted at Wheeling in 1774 -- Ebenezer, Jonathan, Silas, and Andrew Zane and others forted.

General G. R. Clark -- [She] well recollects that George Rogers Clark (so she speaks of him) living about a year at Mr. Conwell's, at the mouth of Fish Creek -- that Clark had a commission sent to him, and then engaged in service. [This residence with Conwell was no doubt in 1773, and perhaps early in 1774. -- L.C.D.] Clark, she says, was a gentleman's son -- had been sent off to try his future in the world -- had his servants with him -- had located a tract of land, near Conwell's, at Fish Creek Flat, and erected on it a cabin, and made a small improvement -- the border troubles coming on prevented further improvements. She says, during the period Clark boarded at Conwell's, he was engaged part of the time in writing -- [he] was a fine young man, and the young men in that region courted his society, and as a recreation, he, at their solicitation, taught them as a kind of family school at Conwell's. [He] often went out hunting, and could not fail to kill turkeys in great plenty.

In 1778, when Clark went down with his men before taking Kaskaskia, he drilled his men at Wheeling, and [they] (one hundred of the men) presented a noble appearance.

FIRST SIEGE OF WHEELING

Of a Monday morning, several cabins outside the fort, Jonathan Zane among them. The first notice of Indians, Dr. McMahon intended to move away, some alarmed. Lieutenant Sam Johnson was applied to for two soldiers to go out and hunt his (McMahon's) horses. John Boyd and one Greathouse went out on the hill-side. [They] were fired on. Boyd was killed and scalped, and Greathouse escaped to the fort. Perhaps a Negro may have been along.

Still thinking it was only a scouting party, Tomlinson and all that could turned out. Greathouse went along to show where Boyd was. [They] found his body. [They] kept along the Indian trail, until around the hill, where the Indians were secreted. [They] rose around them and killed fifteen men, Lieutenant Tomlinson among them. Captain Mason was wounded. Captain Ogle hid in the fence corner (and wounded) and got in [during] the night. This fight was in the morning early. One Harkness fled to Shepherd's Fort. Then the siege commenced.

The people fled from their cabins outside, leaving everything. [They] surrounded the fort and commenced firing on the fort. Colonel Shepherd brought his family [in] the day before. In the afternoon, Francis Duke came along alone on horseback, and came near, when he found the way surrounded. [He] put his horse to his speed, and was shot, but he fell so near [the fort] that they did not get his scalp till evening. [He] dragged his body into a cabin.

Captain Ogle got to Wheeling with his company the day before the siege. In the fight he got wounded and hid in the fence corner; ([she] don't recollect about the rattlesnake) and the second day was discovered and taken in. Captain Mason got his thigh broke. Lieutenant Samuel Tomlinson and fourteen others were killed in the fight or massacre. William Shepherd (son of Col. David Shepherd) was one, and left a wife and child. John Harkness escaped to Shepherd's Fort.

Elizabeth Zane carried powder -- and the balls kicked up the dust around her. She was a cheerful and fearless girl, full of joy, etc. [She] was at Ebenezer [Zane's], outside the fort, and she went and got powder. [She] went to the fort, to the small gate on the creek end. John McCulloch came,

APPENDIX II 105

and [he] was chased, and [he] ran down the hill, saying he knew he would be killed if he fell into the Indians' hands, and [he] could only be killed any way, and [he] went down, and went up the creek. [It was] John McCulloch rode down the hill, as she thinks. No relief [party] of Colonel Swearingen or anyone else at the first siege.

In the evening, the Indians fired the cabins. [They] fired on the fort all night, and next morning, by daylight, they went off. [It was] allowed that Indians were killed, but none [were] found. -- killed, and [a] great deal struck. Not over ten or fifteen fighting men [were left] after Mason's and Ogle's men were defeated. A few men brought in Boyd's body, while the others went on and were attacked. The next day the dead were buried. No British recollected at first siege.

FOREMAN'S DEFEAT

Foreman's and Linn's companies came. Next day [they] went down to see if there was any sign of Indians at Grave Creek, where [there] was a deserted blockhouse. Forty-six turned out to go. [They] camped, [and] next morning Linn, Daniel McLane, and a few others went up the hill, the others marching in Indian file. The Indians had made blinds and were under the river bank, etc., and when the Whites were opposite, Foreman, at the head [of the file], was [the] first shot down, by a single fire. The others stopped suddenly, and were fired on and shot down. McLane said he ran part way down the hill: [he] said he "heard the tomahawks as if the Indians were cutting up beef." [She has] no distinct recollection about Daniel Sullivan, [but] thinks he must have been taken to Shepherd's Fort, as some few families were there still, as Rachael thinks.

In the afternoon, a fugitive with his gun, but without his hat, gave the first mournful intelligence of the defeat, not knowing of any other beside himself who had escaped. Others returned that night, and kept dropping in. Next day a party turned out to bury the dead, etc.

SECOND SIEGE OF WHEELING

With Ebenezer Zane was George Green, Andrew Scott, and young Bob Scott. Molly Scott loaded guns for them. Old Sam in the kitchen was slightly wounded. Captain Pratt and forty British [were present]. Jonathan Zane did speak to Captain Pratt, in the upper river corner bastion. Zane asked Pratt if he was not ashamed to come all the way from Scotland to aid savages in killing women and children. Betsey Wheat cursed them (hearing their fowls squall) for robbing her roosters. Jonathan Zane was asked if he had not a brother among the Indians? Yes, said Zane, and tell him all his brothers here are able, ready, and willing to fight.

[The] Indians were under the bank. [They] threw the gravel over into the fort. [They] throwed stores over, etc. [We] had water heated to scald, in case they attempted to come in. [They] tried to fire the fort, but failed.

Sullivan was wounded that night. [We] fired grape-shot at Rigger's [Reagan's -- L.C.D.] house and drove out the Indians, etc. Two pickets, rotted, fell, etc.

Next morning [a] Negro came in, handcuffed, and Betsey Wheat stood sentry over him with [a] tomahawk. The women stood their tour a part of the day, giving the men by turns a chance for sleep.

The wooden cannon [was fired] in the evening of the second day -- [it was] made of sugar-tree [= maple -- J.C.L.]. The second night the attack was brisk, till day break. [They] left in the morning. The relief arrived under Colonel Williamson, of forty men, from about Washington [Pennsylvania], shortly after the Indians left.

OTHER INFORMATION

Silas Zane and George Green -- Zane took goods to trade with the Indians. [They] sold out, and on return, [they] were both waylaid and killed in the Indian Country.

Lewis Wetzel and another (perhaps young Boggs) tomahawked Kill Buck. Lewis and Jacob were suspected, and were thumbscrewed in a vice, but would not divulge any knowledge. The Indian was placed in his blanket and sunk in the river. [She] thinks this was after George Wetzel had been killed.

# INDEX

ADAMS, John 13
ALEXANDER, Mary 86
AMBERSON, James 101 Mr 34
ANDREW, David 57
ASHBY, Bladen 5 Lt 94
BAKER, 3 Mrs 3
BANE, 94 Capt 5 93
BARNET, Elizabeth Ann 86
BARNETT, 88
BAYLEY, Rachel 86
BEAN, Joseph 93
BEASON, Henry 53
BEE, Bob 92
BEESON, 91 Jacob 91
BIGGS, 24 Capt 20 John 5 93 94 Joseph 22 23 27 Tom 24
BINGAMAN, 19 20 Capt 20 John 19 Mrs 19
BIRD, Col 59
BLACK, 79
BLACKMORE, William 84
BLAIR, 66
BOGGS, 96 106 Capt 96
BONEHAM, Jacob 5
BOONE, 8
BOYD, 104 105 John 104
BRADDOCK, 52 88 103
BRADFORD, 21 David 13 21
BRADLEY, Hannah 86
BRADY, 10 11 18 20-22 27 32-34 38-44 100 101 Capt 10 20 22 26 27 34 38 42-45 Hugh 25 Mr 43 Mrs 21 Samuel 20 34 35 43
BRAZIER, 3 Tom 3

BRENTON, Capt 93
BRICK, James 86 Mary 86
BRODERICK, David 70
BRODHEAD, 12 Col 12
BROWN, Richard 13
BRYANT, 58 60 61 88
BUCK, 38 Joseph 32 34 38 39 100
BUKEY, Dinneen 25 Hezekiah 23
BURKHAM, 95 96 Solomon 91 Stephen 91 95 96
CAHILL, Maj 47
CALLAWAY, Flanders 68
CAMERON, Hugh 92
CAMPBELL, Col 91 James 27
CARNAHAN, 34
CARPENTER, S C 99
CARR, Archibald 96 George 96 Hamilton 95 96
CHAMBERS, 48
CHERRY, Thomas 16
CLARK, 48 103 104 G R 103 Gen 55 96 George Rogers 103
CLOCK, 57
COLEMAN, 73 74
COLLIER, Bates 56
COLVIN, 26 Jacob 26
CONWELL, 103 Yates 103
COX, George 3 25
CRAIG, 83 Absalom 83 Capt 48 John 30 47
CRAWFORD, 2 4 5 9 14 91 93-95 Col 4 57 91 James 57 John 4
CRESAP, Michael 53
CROW, 28 Peter 28

CRUGER, Mrs 95 103
CUMMINS, 89 Susannah 89 Thomas 89
DAVIS, David 25
DEVERS, 54
DEWITT, 60 Ezekiel 97
DICKERSON, 11 Vachel 11
DODDRIDGE, 12 Dr 2 Phil 13
DOWNEY, 60 Mrs 59
DRAPER, 99 Lyman 31 99 Lyman Copeland 29
DUKE, Francis 5 104
DUNBAR, 53 Col 52
DUNMORE, 91 Gov 53 89
DUNN, James 93
EDDY, David 25
EDGINGTON, 1 2 26 27 D M 1 George 1 19 Isaac 25 Joseph 5 27 Mr 2 Thomas 1 2 4 18 21 23 26
EDWARDS, 1
EKELEY, Joseph 57
ELLRED, Elizabeth 78 John Peter 78 Mary 78
ELLROD, Robert 84
ELOT, Peter 52
ENGLE, 3 William 3
FAGAN, 83 Fielding 83
FELTY, Isaac 53
FINCH, 58 61 James 52 John 54 60 61 64 Josiah 60
FINK, David 84
FITCH, 18 John 18
FLINN, 76
FORBES, 103 Capt 23 Gen 20
FOREMAN, 3 91 105
FOX, Arthur 65
FRANTZ, 48
FRY, Henry 59-61 William 57
FULKS, 54
FUSO, Rudolph 78
GAINES, Richard 65
GALLOWAY, Ann 52
GAMMEL, Josiah 57
GARDNER, Abraham 78 John 79
GARRARD, Col 61

GIBSON, Col 3 91
GIRTY, 2 5 7 91 96 George 19 91 96 James 19 Simon 2 19 91
GORDON, John 48
GOSSET, John 69
GRAIG, 47
GREATHOUSE, 3 79 104 Daniel 3
GREEN, 42 96 George 105 106
GREENLEE, James 57
GRIFFITH, William 27
GUTHRIE, 47 Alexander 30 Jack 30 34 James 30 John 30 34
HAINES, Mr 99
HANKS, 6 Peter 6
HANNA, 91
HARKNESS, 104 John 104
HARRISON, 61 Benjamin 61 Maj 93 97 William Henry 61
HARVEY, Elsie 86
HAYS, John 93
HEATON, Elizabeth 86
HECKEWELDER, 2 22
HEDGE, Solomon 24
HENDRICKSON, Josiah 87 Matilda 87
HENRY, Henry 31 Margaret 47 99 Mr 29 30 35 47 49 Peter 29 31 34 35 45 48 49 99
HINKSTON, 59 64
HOOVER, Simeon 40 41
HUBBELL, 79 Capt 79
HUGHEY, Elizabeth 87 John 78 81 82
HUSTON, 64
INDIAN, Bald Eagle 53 Ben Newland 93 Big Foot 17 26 Captain White Eyes 92 Half King 2 16 17 Kill Buck 106 Logan 3 53 Long Pine 10 Queen 2 Scotash 2 17
JACKSON, 16 Philip 16
JANUARY, Thomas 62
JOHNSON, 28 Henry 28 John 28 Rachael 103 105 Sam 104
JOHNSTON, 80 Dr 77
KELLOGG, Louise Phelps 99

# INDEX

KELLY, 6
KENTON, 14 74 78 Gen 74 John 70 77 78 81 Simon 61 73
KILPATRICK, 79
KIMBERLEY, John 24
KING, 3 Edward 3
KINNEY, Daniel 18
KIRKPATRICK, 48 Mr 48
KISER, 58-60 62 John 58
KNIGHT, Dr 5 95
LAMB, 97
LAUGHERY, 55 Capt 54 55
LEE, 68 69 73 81 82 Capt 81
LEFLER, 95
LEWIS, 72 Col 84 Ezekiel 30 John 72
LINN, 24 91 105 William 91
LOCHRY, Col 30
LORD, Dickson 72
MACHIR, 71 John 71
MADDEN, Thomas 27
MADISON, 11 12
MAHAFFY, 48 John 48
MARSHALL, 65 77 Thomas 76
MARSHEL, James 92 96
MARTIN, 59
MASON, 5 105 Capt 3 104 Isaac 3 John 3 Samuel 3
MASTERS, Lot 69
MAY, 76 John 76
MCCANDLESS, Alexander 55
MCCLELLAN, 93
MCCLELLING, Alexander 64 William 61
MCCONNEL, 63 Alister 62
MCCONNELL, 60 Alexander 61
MCCULLOCH, 6 23 24 94 Capt 23 24 John 6 23 92 94 104 105 Maj 6 Samuel 6 94
MCDONALD, 54 91
MCGINNIS, William 83
MCGUIRE, 13 27 Francis 27 94 Maj 13 27
MCINTOSH, 91 92 Gen 87 91
MCLANE, Daniel 105
MCMAHON, 23 104 Dr 104 Maj 23 William 23

MCNEELY, Alexander 55 56 James 55 56
MEEK, Mrs 55
MEEKS, 71 Jeremiah 71
MIFFLIN, Gov 27
MILLER, 14-16 26 John 26 Mr 48
MILLS, 5 10 94 95 Thomas 4 9
MITCHELL, 24 28 Alex 22-24 Alexander 28
MOHR, Christopher 13
MOORE, 6
MORGAN, 7
MORRIS, 69
MORRISON, 23 William 23
MOSSIE, Gen 85
MUNN, 94 Capt 93
MURPHY, Daniel 30
NEGRO, 19 96 97 104 106 Old Sam 97 105
NEISINGER, 95 Peter 95
NELSON, Milton I 87 Rachel 87
NICHOLSON, 42 101 Mr 34 39 41 47 Thomas 4
OGLE, 105 Capt 104 Joseph 94 Thomas 94
OLNEY, John S 30
ORR, 99 Robert 29
OVERFIELD, Abner 66
PAINTER, Jacob 48
PARCHMENT, Peter 34
PARKINSON, Joseph 15
PARKMAN, 101
PATTERSON, 26 27 Gen 26 Thomas 26
PERRY, 35
PETER, 64
PETERS, 57
PETTEE, Dr 10
PIATT, Benjamin 12
POE, 2 16 17 Adam 17 Andrew 16 17 Captain 16 17
POMEROY, Col 30 46 47
POWELL, 71
PRATT, 91 96 Capt 91 105
PUGH, 3 Jonathan 3
QUATURMOS, 53
QUICK, Susannah 86 Tunis 86

QUOTERMOS, 52 James 52
RALPH, 54 55 Ephraim 54
RANKIN, 20 Col 78 80
REA, 99 Samuel J 99
REAGAN, 106
REARDON, Daniel 56
RECORDS, 77 Ann 52 Capt 54 73
   83 Elizabeth 78 86 87 Elizabeth
   Ann 86 Elsie 86 Hannah 86
   Isaiah 86 James 86 John 52 65
   86 87 Joseph 87 Josiah 51 52 87
   90 Laban 72 75 77-84 86 87
   Lucinda 87 Mary 86 87 90
   Matilda 87 Nicy 87 Rachel 86 87
   Sarah 87 Spencer 51 52 87
   Susanna 52 57 Susannah 86 87
   William 86 87
REDICK, Mr 34 46
REEVES, 60
RICE, 7 97
RICKARDS, William 25
RIDDELL, 59
RIGGER, 106 Anthony 96 Jacob 97
ROBERTS, James 74
ROBERTSON, 53 57 64
ROSE, 94 Ezekiel 93
ROSS, James 21
SAPPINGTON, John 3
SCOTT, Andrew 96 105 Bob 105
   George 96 Molly 105
SELLERS, Isaac 75
SHANE, 65 69
SHANKS, 65
SHEPHERD, 104 105 Col 104
   David 92 104 Moses 97 Wm 104
SHERLOCK, 18 Edward 18 Ned 18
SHERROD, William 27
SHIRER, 55 Robert 55
SHOOT, Philip 53
SLOAN, John 30
SLOVER, 5 20 John 4
SMITH, 68 Henry 95 Jacob 34 43
   45 Mr 44
SPRIGGS, 19
SPROUL, Hugh 74 Jane 74
STALLIONS, John 54
STEVENSON, 18 George 19

STOCKTON, 69
STONER, 59 61 64 78 80 Mr 99
STOUP, Conrad 96
STRONG, Col 11
STROUD, 69
SULLIVAN, 96 106 Daniel 96 105
SUTHERLAND, 24 John 24
SWEARINGEN, Andrew 94 Capt
   21 Col 105 Ms 21
TALMAGE, Thomas 69
TATE, 97 John 96
THOMAS, 68
THOMPSON, Zachariah 70
TODD, Col 67
TOMLINSON, 104 Samuel 104
TUCKER, 79
TULLY, Susan 52
TURNER, 54 58 Betsey 55 George
   55 William 55
ULIN, Ben 95
VANBUSKIRK, 22 25 Lawrence 23
   25 Mrs 26 Mrs Lawrence 26
VANMETER, 6 94
VANSWEARINGEN, 3 Capt 21
VIRGIN, Reason 92
WALKER, Col 30
WALLACE, 92 Robert 19
WALLIS, 34 45 46 Richard 30
   Richard 34
WASHBURN, Cornelius 13
WASHINGTON, 103 George 18
   President 13
WATSON, James 24
WAYNE, 18
WELCH, William 92
WELLS, Thomas 27 Tom 27
WETZEL, 7-11 13-15 24 28 94
   George 7 9 14 15 106 Jacob 7-9
   12-14 16 24 28 95 106 John 7 9
   14 15 22 95 Lewis 4 7-16 27 94
   95 106 Martin 7 8 16
WHEAT, Betsey 96 105 106
WILKEY, 47
WILLIAMS, 71 James 25
WILLIAMSON, 5 18 92-94 Col 56
   92 93 97 106 Col D 93 David 19
   Eleazar 93 John 22

WILSON, 46 Amos 64 Hannah 86
  John 83 86 Maj 30 34 45-47
WITHERS, 25
WOOD, Hezekiah 69 William 65
WOODS, 73 83 Amos 73 Henry 83
  John 57 71 Tobias 73 83
WRIGHT, Joseph 72 Solomon 96

ZANE, 5 6 24 25 84 85 97 105 106
  Andrew 96 103 Col 5 Ebenezer
  12 95 96 103-105 Elizabeth 94
  104 Isaac 24 Jonathan 4 95 103-
  105 Ms 6 Silas 96 103 106
----, John 58 Josiah 58

www.ingramcontent.com/pod-product-compliance
Lightning Source LLC
Chambersburg PA
CBHW050648160426
43194CB00010B/1857